THE ARTICULATE EXECUTIVE IN ACTION:

How The Best Leaders Get Things Done

Other books by Granville Toogood:

The Articulate Executive—Learn to Look, Act, and Sound Like a Leader

The Inspired Executive—The Art of Leadership

The Creative Executive—How Business Leaders Innovate by Stimulating Passion, Intuition, and Creativity

THE ARTICULATE EXECUTIVE IN ACTION:

How The Best Leaders Get Things Done

Granville N. Toogood

McGraw-Hill
New York Chicago San Francisco Lisbon London
Madrid Mexico City Milan New Delhi San Juan Seoul
Singapore Sydney Toronto

The *McGraw-Hill* Companies

1 2 3 4 5 6 7 8 9 0   DOC/DOC   0 9 8 7 6 5

ISBN 0-07-145788-7

McGraw-Hill books are available at special quantity discounts to use as premiums and sales promotions, or for use in corporate training programs. For more information, please write to the Director of Special Sales, Professional Publishing, McGraw-Hill, Two Penn Plaza, New York, NY 10121-2298. Or contact your local bookstore.

 This book is printed on recycled, acid-free paper containing a minimum of 50% recycled, de-inked fiber.

I dedicate this book to my
angel and wisest advisor,
my wife Pat.

CONTENTS

Preface   ix

Acknowledgments   xiii

PART I: Start Your Engines

Chapter 1: In the Driver's Seat   3

Chapter 2: CVA: High Octane for the Fast Track   7

Chapter 3: Getting Up to Speed: The Seven Principles of CVA
    19

Chapter 4: Stepping on the Gas: Adding POWER   27

Chapter 5: Lapping the Field   35

Chapter 6: The 50 Percent Solution: Filling Potholes in Your
    Career Path   41

PART II: The Race

Chapter 7: First, Go for the Gut   49

Chapter 8: Fast Starts and Smart Charts   57

Chapter 9: How Leaders Drive the Message   63

Chapter 10: Putting the Team in the Passing Lane   73

Chapter 11: Speed Bumps—A Cautionary Tale   77

Chapter 12: Fuel Injection   83

Chapter 13: Who's Driving?   89

Chapter 14: The Winner's Circle   95

Chapter 15: Fire Control   101

PART III: Rules of the Road

Chapter 16: Taking the Pole Position   111

Chapter 17: Up to Speed: Fuzzballs and Hardballs   121

Chapter 18: Staying Ahead of the Pack: The 8-Second Rule and 18-Minute Wall   127

Chapter 19: On the Inside Track: Leading by Example   133

Chapter 20: Staying Ahead: How to Leverage Language   139

Chapter 21: How to Avoid the Crash and Burn   149

Chapter 22: The Last Lap   163

Checklist   167
Index   173
About the Author   178

PREFACE

FIRST

The future belongs to the flexible, the creative, and those with a talent for working well with other people. Clever software and technology will inevitably claim jobs of a predictable and repetitive nature. But in the end, we—not our inventions—will be masters and builders of our own destinies. People invent new technologies, build new industries, run new companies, champion new ideas, and engage in time-honored rituals of human interaction and communication that feed growth and drive waves of revolutionary change. History bears witness that the greater the challenge, the more forceful the response. Entrepreneurs, visionaries, innovators, educators, consultants, managers, inventors, designers, and decision makers from every stripe of life will lead the way. Contrary to some pundits' prognostications, the twenty-first century will not be hostage to technology. We will still need leaders, and those leaders will still have to articulate the endless paths, visions, directions, and dreams that create the jobs that create the new technologies that create the jobs that create the visions that build the future of the world. It is to these men and women of the future that I dedicate this book.

WHO'S THE LEADER?

One of the undeniable benefits of being reasonably smart and talented is the likelihood that you will eventually rise to some level of responsibility. That level is often self-fulfilling, depending on the circumstances, and the place where most people spend their entire careers. From this productive—if not entirely fulfilled—pool of people will invariably rise, one by one, a handful of achievers. A few will be so smart that the premium value on their services will propel them upward in spite of themselves. Others will succeed on charm and political skill alone. Neither is likely to make it all the way to the top. The top slots are reserved for just a few players. This select group distinguishes itself not only with brains, talent, and varying degrees of charm but also with the single characteristic that others lack: passion—and a desire to share that passion with others. These people are all on a *mission*.

These select few share another trait: They understand that leadership manifests in *action*, not *position*. They know that it isn't about what we are but what we do.

We all know people who are supposed to be running things but, in fact, merely occupy the corner office. By contrast, the authentic leader takes his or her identity not from a title and its trappings but from decisions that spur action. To show solidarity with his people and indifference toward token symbols of power, the true leader might even shun the executive suite in favor of a modest office or even a "bullpen." New York Mayor Bloomberg, a one-time Wall Street whiz and founder of the

Bloomberg Networks, is one such leader. In fact, entrepreneurs as a group often make a point of showing they are not impressed by the perks of power. They are saying, in effect, know me by my actions. Let my leadership speak for itself.

We all know people who have a talent for finance, or organizational skills, or manufacturing, operations, strategies, tactics, and the rest. But these talents of and by themselves do not a leader make.

Leadership in business begins outside the corner office.

Intuitive leaders get out of the corner office and down on the shop floor and talk to their people. Leaders are the first to step forward, the first to take a position. Leaders don't pass the buck to the PR flack. Leaders speak personally for the company or the team. Leaders are the first to draw the line and the first to step over the line.

The great leader will put his company, employees, customers, and investors ahead of himself, and the legendary leader will find a way to serve them all.

Passionate leaders who can articulate that passion create passionate followers. This wave of focus and commitment can push profit, cut costs, and fuel the engines of growth and prosperity.

In *The Articulate Executive*, I talked about competence, clarity, and communication. If you are reasonably good at what you do, clearly articulate your ideas to all audiences, and know how to deliver your message so that people remember it and act on it, you can call yourself a leader. Add integrity, courage, commitment, and vision, and you can call yourself a worthy leader.

In this book I put the emphasis on how to apply the principles of *The Articulate Executive* to your daily professional life. Regardless of your pursuit, regardless of your rank or experience, think of this book as a kind of a key to an exclusive club. The members of this club are the celebrated leaders of our time and every time. Read on.

ACKNOWLEDGMENTS

I would like to thank Alex Hiam for his clever mind, unflagging sense of fun, and masterly grasp of the sometimes daunting, ever-challenging process of creation. And hats off once again to Pat, my wife, best friend, and closest advisor. Also to my kids, Heather and Chase, who have now produced their own miracles: Gigi, Talmadge, Charlotte, and Grayson.

START YOUR ENGINES

IN THE DRIVER'S SEAT

A CEO of a Forbes 100 company gets up to speak to his first analyst meeting. By the time he sits down, he has done his company more harm than good. The next day, the stock falls, leaving the CEO shocked and frustrated.

The new marketing executive vice president of a large consumer products company calls for action at the annual corporate conference but generates only yawns and inaction.

A department head convenes her troops in an effort to increase productivity. She tries her best to persuade, but two days later nobody can pass a quiz on what she said. Nor do they seem to care.

A newly minted MBA is called into an important meeting to help close on a big transaction worth millions, but he drops the ball so badly the deal is lost.

A team leader holds his first meeting with his team and comes away with the feeling that even though he felt that he said and did everything right, the whole meeting seemed to go wrong.

These true snapshots constitute only a tiny peek under the tent at a huge and troubling secret hiding behind the closed doors of corporate America: Companies large and small are filled with smart, competent, even talented people who can't get things done.

That's because they don't connect. They don't know how to get people to do what they want them to do. Nor do they know how to advance their product, their services, or themselves. This costs all of us—customers, employees, and investors alike—because lackluster leadership (or even the perception of lackluster leadership) often results in indifference. Indifference invariably leads to mediocrity. Mediocrity invariably leads to poor results. For most people, poor results can mean sinking sales, sagging market share, loss of business, erosion of jobs, and the disappearance of investment dollars.

> **Indifference invariably leads to mediocrity. Mediocrity invariably leads to poor results.**

The answer is so disarmingly simple, most people don't believe it when they hear it. Actually, the answer is threefold. Great leadership requires (1) an idea or vision and the singlemindedness to back it up, (2) a solid understanding of human nature and how to appeal to that human nature, and (3) inspiration—and this can be either an intuitive knowledge of how to capture people's minds and hearts or, more often than not, a kind of charismatic skill that can actually be learned.

Knowledge of management skills, strategies, tactics, operations, manufacturing, marketing, sales, finance, and ethics is important. But any good leader knows that if his own people can't steer a meeting, command a stage, negotiate a transaction, understand their own message, sell product or service, or persuade others to follow, then these people are consistently coming up short and often leaving money on the table—again to the detriment of employees, customers, investors, and themselves.

The problem is what we might call the gap between good intentions and actuality. *Good intentions* means that we assume everybody shares our views, that they're all on board. It means we assume they're motivated and that everything will be fine.

But the *actuality* is often very different. The actuality may well be that nobody has a clue where you're going with the company or what you expect them to do to help you get there. They're not on board (because the train isn't even in the station), and they're not motivated (why should they be?).

A leadership vacuum can pop the potential of any company. If you are the energy and your people are the battery, that battery will go flat and eventually die without periodic recharging from the energy source. Nothing could be more obvious, yet too few leaders recognize this simple truth. One who does is long-time advertising guru Charlotte Beers, who says that the first job of the CEO (or any leader) is to have a vision. The second job is to push that vision all the way from the board room to the mail room or wherever it has to go to make sure things happen.

Do you have a vision? You might think you do. But do you know how to articulate that vision so that others will follow? Can you make a believer out of the disbeliever? Can you make things happen?

Do you really understand to whom you speak? Are you alert to their hopes and fears and deepest needs?

Can you get your people up out of their chairs and out of the room to do exactly what you want them to do? (This is a talent Sun Microsystems CEO Scott McNeely calls "getting all the wood behind the arrrowhead.")

Some very competent businesspeople will tell you, in confidence, "No," to all the preceding. These are people who, in their own view and by their own reckoning, will admit to being better managers than leaders. Some are even content to think of themselves as functionaries. I know any number of engineers, accountants, civil servants, and administrators running whole departments in both the public and private sectors who simply manage and are happy to do so until their last working day.

With all due respect to the good men and women who labor admirably long and hard in their various fields, the inevitable consequence of mere management is, of course, a strong bias toward the middle.

But on the fiercely competitive corporate and entrepreneurial playing fields where most of us compete every day, a consistent bias toward the middle can be the first step toward losing the game.

You can avoid that bias toward the middle by taking out an insurance policy I call *CVA*.

CVA: HIGH OCTANE FOR THE FAST TRACK

A Yankelovich survey found that if you compare two blue chip companies of roughly equal size and reputation, the one with a dynamic leader will typically have a market value of as much as 50 percent above the company without dynamic leadership. So all things being equal, leadership by itself can be shown to be the trump card in every company's future, accounting for perhaps billions of dollars in added value. (If the two companies were to swap CEOs, would the numbers reverse themselves? The survey doesn't speculate.)

The Yankelovich survey underscores an often-overlooked phenomenon I only half-jokingly call *communications value added* (CVA) (half-jokingly because we already have EVA—economic value added—and MVA—market value added—and the last thing we need, it seems to me, is another value added).

> **If a leader with good business sense and a great idea or a solid sense of direction can talk the talk, that company will prosper.**

CVA is just another way of defining a key characteristic of leadership. In full flower, CVA is the difference between a company that's on fire and a company that's asleep. But it's not taught in any business schools. CVA says that what you say and how you say it can determine the success of your business. If a leader with good business sense and a great idea or a solid sense of direction can talk the talk—charm Wall Street, inspire employees, reassure shareholders, manipulate the press to good advantage, win friends and influence people—that company will prosper.

But no one should be intimidated by CVA. It's as available and natural as the sun coming up in the morning. Virtually anybody can practice CVA.

Once you get the hang of it, CVA can become your greatest asset. One of the first business leaders to recognize the value of CVA was Lee Iacocca, the former Chrysler chairman (before the company merger with Daimler-Benz). Iacocca knew that if he didn't personally come forward, the company might die. First, he went to Congress and persuaded the government to give him a fat loan. Next, he went to the American people (via TV and commercials) and told them, "If you can find a better car for the price, buy it." He made believers out of disbelievers. People bought Chrysler cars—in spite of poor quality and poor reliability—and that's arguably the only reason you can still buy a Jeep today.

Before he stepped down at General Electric (GE), Jack Welch knew the future of GE rested on a man or woman, like himself, who would come across as an articulate leader.

"I want somebody with incredible energy who can excite others," he said. "I want somebody who can *define their vision* [the emphasis is mine], who finds change fun and doesn't get paralyzed by it. I want somebody who feels comfortable in Delhi or Denver. I mean, somebody who really feels comfortable and can talk to all kinds of people."

In other words, somebody with CVA.

When he talked to his own people, Jack always had the same message: "The only one who can guarantee you have a job is a satisfied customer." That single sentence alone is the catalyst behind two decades of double-digit revenue growth at GE under Welch's stewardship.

Even years after retirement, Welch was still waxing wide-eyed about how business leaders should demonstrate "a passion to get great people" into management positions and "an inordinate desire to want to win in the global world . . . always trying to raise the intellectual bar of a company, looking everywhere for ideas."

You don't have to look far to see why Welch is still celebrated as a visionary and a man who knows how to get things done.

Jack's successor, Jeff Immelt, turned out to be as comfortable and, arguably, as passionate as his predecessor. He is equally at home sharing his vision with employees, customers, analysts, and talk-show hosts.

Immelt's views of GE's place in the world differ from his predecessor's. Instead of growth by acquisition, for instance, he is betting the farm on internal growth and reorganizing the company to be less dependent on the economy and market cycles.

You can sum up his message to his people in one sentence: *From now on, we depend on ourselves for our own growth.*

When employees hear this message, they see that they are part of something bigger than themselves and want to participate in GE's next success story.

To outside audiences, Immelt talks about GE in almost mystical terms. He tells an audience at MIT, for example, " . . . It's really a story about faith . . . a big company with conviction, with speed, can change the world in a way that others can't."

He's the head coach of one of the oldest, biggest, and most admired companies in the world. Yet he worships innovation, thinks like an entrepreneur, and knows that it will take inspired leadership to stay on top in the twenty-first century.

"Good leaders prepare the organization to innovate," he says. "They really put a focus on people and process and culture to make sure that their companies are great places to work. Good leaders pick the right places to innovate. They develop a nose for big changes, and they're willing to put big levels of resources behind that change. Good leaders know how to make innovation pay for investors, making the rewards match the risk and putting the resources at the right place at the right time. And good leaders, particularly in companies like GE, know how to use size as an advantage and never let it be a disadvantage."

Importantly, like any great leader, he is comfortable with change.

"In the late '90s we became business traders and not business growers. . . . the capital market dominated. . . . it was all about how you flip things to capitalize on what was going on in the commercial markets. . . . today, organic growth is the key. . . . it's going to determine who gets rewarded, and is absolutely the biggest task of every company."

The great leader sets goals:

"We made the central question that every [GE] CEO had to answer when they came to their strategic plan is, 'What will it take for my product or source to be a technical leader, to be the value leader in our industry?'"

He understands the global market:

"We found multiple ways to accelerate our technology and get faster to market. The way we did that was we globalized more. We opened up research centers in Bangalore, Shanghai, and Munich. We did it to have access to markets. But we also did it to get access to the best brains anywhere in the world."

Above all, great leaders are passionate:

"We made innovation exciting and fun," he tells the MIT audience. "We redid a 23-year-old slogan called, 'We bring goods things to life,' and replaced it with a slogan called, 'Imagination at work.' And what that did more than anything else is speak to the culture of who we wanted to be. We wanted people to bring their brain; we wanted people to think that GE was a place where dreams could become reality. That was what could differentiate us. Now we're backing that up with funding 50 imagination projects within the company that are going to get corporate support, that are driving organic growth.

"My story on preparing an organization to innovate isn't about skunk works and heroes," he says. "We prepare GE to innovate by making it central to our leadership process, by making it the expectation of leadership. Our leaders know that the businesses have to change. Ultimately, I think the leaders of the future are going to have three traits: They're going to have a sense for the external markets, they're going to have a great fingertip touch with technology, and they're going to understand ways to do that every place in the world."

Is there any doubt in your mind about where this man is going?

Put it all together, and investors, customers, and employees all get a sense that Immelt is the right man in the right place at the right time. He knows he's got a good story to tell—after all, he helped create it—and he's leveraging that story as a valuable business tool to anyone who's willing to listen.

"The headlines of the future are all going to be about the changes that are being driven today," he says. "I really believe when I look at leaders, there are two things I admire. One is the absolute courage and willingness to drive change, to do it through thick and thin and be willing to stand behind it. The other one is a sense of optimism. The fact is that cynics don't make investments, right? Cynics don't hire people. Cynics don't create wealth. This is a world for optimists. It's a world for change, and it's a world for optimism. It's my plan that GE is always in the lead."

This is how the great leader articulates his vision—the head coach in full flower, driving up the market value of his company almost every time he opens his mouth.

But even otherwise unremarkable people can harness CVA to stunning advantage. For example, Remington Electric Shavers went from a close shave with bankruptcy to a household name with the help of the company's owner, Victor Kiam, who served as Remington's on-air spokesman for years.

Sy Syms speaks like a Harvard don as he hawks his bargain-basement garments. His line is something like, "Our best customer is an educated consumer." People start buying the line and then start buying the clothes. Syms parlays his minor celebrity and smooth voice into a booming business in the New York area.

That's CVA.

A man named David Orrick enthusiastically pitches his industrial-strength vacuum cleaners on the radio and cleans up big time.

That's CVA.

Mort Lebenthal increased his bond-trading firm's business fivefold by getting out of the corner office and into people's cars and homes. He simply buys airtime on the radio and does the commercials himself. Mort's a true believer. True believers are the best persuaders. Mort— and now his daughter—seem to have no trouble persuading people that Lebenthal is the answer to their future financial security. This is added business that the Lebenthals might never have realized had Mort not recognized the value of CVA (even though he may not have known what to call it).

Today a lot of people think of Martha Stewart as a convicted corporate crook. But the story of her rise before the fall should serve as an inspiration to anyone looking to be successful in business.

Martha seized on CVA right from the start, rapidly parlaying a vision, hard work, fresh understanding of an entire market, knowledge, an easy style, good looks, and natural charm into a multibillion-dollar domestic lifestyle and self-help business. Martha capitalized with characteristic passion and unflagging energy in an untapped niche market, the American homemaker, who was more than ready to follow her lead and buy her products. The market was ready, Martha was able and decidedly willing—and the rest is history.

Her mantra became a clarion call to women all over America. Through her wildly popular magazines, tapes, DVDs, books, and radio and TV shows, she became the master of multimedia CVA, which boiled down to just one simple message repeated a million times in five years: "You can learn something new from Martha every day." Millions of women loved the message and loved Martha. They opened their wallets and became devotees in the church of Martha Stewart Living.

She wound up a self-made billionaire, and a lot of people believe that had it not been for her conviction for lying to prosecutors over a stock sale, and prison time, she could have gone even farther. But even as she faced incarceration, she found an opportunity to calm the concerns of her fans, customers, partners, employees, and investors and help to protect her company during her absence by holding a news conference:

"I know I have a very tough five months ahead of me," she said. "But I understand, too, that I will get through those months knowing that I have the ability to return to my productive and normal life, my interesting work and future business opportunities, supported through the ordeal by my friends and colleagues and loved ones. I am very sad knowing that I will miss the holiday season. Halloween, Thanksgiving, Christmas, and New Year's are always opportunities to celebrate family, friends, and religious traditions that mean so much to many of us. And I will miss all of my pets, my two beloved, fun-loving dogs, my seven lively cats, my canaries, my horses, and even my chickens. . . .

"I would like to be back as early in March as possible in order to plant the new spring garden and to truly get things growing again. . . .

"I know I have the full support of the management team and the board of directors going forward through this period. . . .

"I hope that by ending the uncertainty and the awkwardness and the awfulness we can return to better times quickly and efficiently. I cannot express enough gratitude to my family, my friends, both old and new, coworkers and business partners and, of course, the millions of fans who have written and e-mailed me countless encouraging notes, watched our shows, read our magazines and books, purchased our products and supported our brands."

In other words, Martha is saying: "Don't go away—I'll be right back!"

Fans, customers, suppliers, investors, and employees all took comfort. After a brief falter, her company stock bounced back. When she got out of jail, she hit the ground running and started making up for lost time. For that, she can thank her high-octane CVA.

Sometimes it's amazing what a little CVA can do. Even the most unlikely people can suddenly burst from years of shell-bound confinement, given the opportunity.

To my surprise and delight, I discovered that a bespectacled and introverted CFO of a major investment bank jumped at the chance to have a little fun as one of the key presenters at the bank's annual managing directors' conference.

It turned out to be an epiphany.

For years, his greatest fear was public speaking. He lost sleep just thinking about presentations. But with a little encouragement, once we started putting his big conference presentation together it was he—not I—who began coming up with the good ideas and catchy one-liners. He even created a skit, which required him to dress up as a Roman. He taped this skit with the head of operations, who also dressed as a Roman. The result was a hit with the audience. Importantly, the entertainment value did not come at the expense of the business message.

The result was ironic. Some people lose their personalities onstage, but my client actually found himself transformed, both personally and professionally. He gained confidence in meetings and presentations. His peers and his reports began to see him in an entirely different light.

Dread turned to delight, and months later both he and his coworkers were telling me he was a changed man.

CVA is the extra business that personal connection can bring to any transaction. (That's why God created golf—it's arguably true that more deals are hatched, more alliances formed, more sales realized, and more business concluded on golf courses than in all the conference rooms in the world.)

CVA is the winning factor that can put a shaky deal over the top. (Just one phone call from the right person at the right time or a brief private huddle of key players can rescue even the most tenuous of negotiations.)

CVA is the difference between a tiresome presentation and a jolt of enlightenment. (Hundreds of billions of dollars of opportunity are lost each year to confusion, indifference, or boredom arising from crummy communication.)

CVA is the glue that makes it possible for individuals and teams to work more productively. (An inspired captain of any team can extract an uncommon performance from common people.)

CVA is the catalyst that helps to create change, promotes profit, and generates acceptance for unpopular measures such as cost cutting. (When organizations understand why bad things sometimes happen to good people, evolution can occur.)

CVA is the largely unrecognized critical component that can spell the difference between success and failure. In other words, CVA is what it takes to make things happen. And CVA can make a difference in every corner of business—from presentations to e-mails to mentoring to negotiation to conflict resolution to sales, marketing, corporate communications, investors relations, and much more.

And at the top, as I noted, a leader with CVA can eclipse the competition. At this level it is almost impossible to measure its actual value.

The dark side of CVA is that it can equally well serve greed and outrageous self-aggrandizement. Take the case of Bernie Ebbers, a onetime basketball coach from Mississippi who had a telecom vision that he single-handedly sold to investors with a beguiling mix of country smarts and old boy charm. A lot of sophisticated investors fell for Bernie's line and then watched in horror as the whole house of cards, which eventually came to be known as WorldCom, came crashing down around their heads. Ebbers was convicted and was awaiting a June 13, 2005 sentencing.

Or look at Dennis Koslowski, the disgraced and indicted former chairman of Tyco, who went on a five-year acquisition binge with the help of bankers and financial service pros too easily impressed by Koslowski's brains and considerable powers of persuasion. The whole thing was built on a soft berm of massive debt. According to prosecutors, once the borrowed money started rolling in, Koslowski lost no time getting his hand in the cookie jar and looting Tyco to the tune of $600 million. He avoided potential conviction after his case ended in mistrial in April, 2004.

And how about Andrew Fastow, the articulate, razor-sharp, facile, and financially talented former CFO of Enron, who is serving 10 years in a federal pen for cooking the books, creating diabolically ingenious scam transactions on a huge scale, and an assortment of other crimes and misdemeanors.

Then there's former Health South CEO Richard Scrushy, who was charged with masterminding a $2.7 billion dollar accounting fraud to mislead investors.

These four white-collar renegades, and a host of others, could never have climbed as high as they did had they not understood, perhaps better than most, the power of CVA not only to bend wills and muscle change but also to warp reality. History is full of dark personalities who wielded CVA to poisonous effect, including Hitler, Mussolini, Stalin, Bob Jones (the mad cult leader who ordered his followers to commit suicide by drinking cyanide-laced Kool-Aid), Saddam Hussein, and most insidious of all, the disarmingly soft-spoken Osama Bin Laden, whose message of intolerance, murder, genocide, and mass destruction is cleverly masked in talk of God backed by a gentle expression and ecclesiastical robes (he makes a cruelly ironic point of projecting a Christlike image).

History is also rich with towering figures who embraced CVA for the greater good, including Christ, Mohammed, Gandhi, and a whole raft of prophets large and small.

If CVA can change the world, it can certainly help grow your business.

GETTING UP TO SPEED: THE SEVEN PRINCIPLES OF CVA

The first principle of CVA is to never bore.

At a conference in Dallas, a highly regarded research director for a consumer products company gives a lengthy presentation reading from a prepared text and leaves his audience feeling short-changed. They had expected a lot more, frankly, than what they got. During a break, an attendee is overheard whispering how tedious she thought the research director was. And not only the research director but also his presentation. Later he gets the lowest speaker rating at the confab.

A thousand miles away in Chicago, a software marketing executive visits a prospective client to try to get new business. The meeting takes place in a conference room where the marketing executive starts out by saying how much she appreciates having the opportunity to make this presentation. Then she starts reading the agenda.

Already the prospective clients are looking at their watches. It's eight minutes into the presentation, and they're still waiting for the bottom line. They haven't heard anything interesting or even useful yet, and at this rate, it doesn't look like they will.

This presentation sinks into a stifling cloud of white noise that effectively turns everybody off. It winds up going nowhere and getting nothing accomplished. A waste of time for everybody in the room. The Q&A goes a little better because the marketing executive comes to life, but it's too little and too late, and the sale never happens.

Twenty minutes later a senior sales executive from another competing software company walks in, and the room seems to light up. It's not that she has charisma. But she's outgoing, friendly, and clearly accessible, and you get the feeling that she didn't come here to lay a big presentation on you but rather to have a conversation—and that's exactly what happens.

She starts off without notes or presentation book, her laptop closed, telling a little story about how she'd run into somebody on the plane who also happened to be a customer. It turns out the customer was returning from a business trip of his own. When he discovered which company she worked for, he launched into a remarkable tribute about how her software, a sophisticated back office management package, had been the decisive factor in convincing a group of venture capitalists (VCs) to take a minority stake in his company. That minority stake was the company's last hope for survival. The VCs confided that it was the quality and reliability of the software suite that helped them to justify the risk and tipped the decision to buy.

She says that she's running into this kind of enthusiastic reaction everywhere she goes and offers to show them what all the buzz is about. She takes a risk of her own and runs a demo of the software in real time (fortunately, the laptop and hookups work without a flaw).

By now the listeners are fully engaged. The software demo is brief but impressive. The woman is on a roll. Everybody's paying attention, and nobody's looking at their watch.

Best of all, she's not talking about how cool the software design and engineering are. She doesn't have to; the demo says it all. What she's talking about is what they want to hear: She's telling them how this software can make them money and save money. It's all about how it can benefit their business, and she's boned up enough on their company so that she can talk about hypothetical applications with specific business issues they can relate to.

Before she's even finished, they all know who's going to get this assignment. She can sense it, too, and there's a kind of optimism and excitement in the room that wasn't there before.

Her clients have dodged the dreaded boredom bullet, and they are prepared to reward her for sparing them.

In business, being boring carries consequences. Being boring can have an adverse effect on your ability to lead, which, in turn, can affect your relationships with clients, peers, employees, and shareholders.

If you wind up at the top and you bore, you could also wind up presiding over the decline of your company.

The second principle of CVA is always leave people with more when they walk out than when they walked in. While the research director is boring people in Dallas, an information technology officer is droning through a different but equally insipid presentation in Boston. He's plowing through the entire process that led up to the selection of certain software and hardware and then spends what seems like ages reviewing the finer points of the actual technologies themselves, even showing schematics and discussing itemized platform features, sometimes 20 or 30 to a page. On top of that, he's throwing arcane acronyms around like they were confetti, and you'd almost need a translator to understand the technobabble.

His audience of department heads, middle managers, and sales associates doesn't get it. What they want to know is, What will this stuff do for me? Why is it better than what I've got now? Is it easy to use? Is there adequate backup in the system and support in the program? Instead, they're getting a lecture on the design process and a detailed look at the technology. Some technophiles in the audience are fascinated. But the speaker goes so long that there's no time for Q&A, and the vast majority walks out the door feeling they've gained nothing. They, too, feel short-changed.

The third principle of CVA is always be master of your presentation—never allow your presentation to master you. In San Francisco, a newly appointed vice president of marketing at a promising Silicon Valley startup mounts the stage at his first investors' meeting. He takes his position behind the lectern, turns down the house lights, puts up a big slide with lots of sentences, and starts reading from the slide. He reads from the next slide, and the next, and the next. His audience is wondering, Why did this guy bother to show up? Why didn't he just send a memo? A memo would have been a lot more useful. At this point they're thinking, What would happen if this guy were suddenly denied his word slides? Would he still know what to say?

The vice president has become a slave to his own presentation, a bottom-lit talking head who seems to add no value by his actual presence on the stage. The investors feel frustrated because they want to see their management in action to get a better sense of what kind of people (read leaders) they are. Right now they're not getting a particularly good feeling about this vice president.

The fourth principle of CVA is to speak only about what you know. At an industry conference in Philadelphia, the CEO of a regional real estate development company is asked to speak on executive development. It's a subject that he has a passing acquaintance with but no particular interest, insights, or knowledge, save for some personal computer tutoring he received a few years back. Still, he figures the conference is in his own back yard, and it might generate business. So he asks his human resources person to prepare his remarks.

When the CEO shows up at the conference, the organizers tell him that he will be sitting on a panel. It turns out two of the three other guest speakers are executive education experts. When his turn comes, he reads his remarks verbatim from beginning to end, which compares poorly with the other speakers, who know their subject cold, require no notes, and provide fresh ideas, insight, and inspiration. The real-life stories they tell from their own experience resonate with the audience. When the panelists take questions, he feels unprepared and painfully inadequate compared with the others. He's beginning to wonder if he's done himself and his company more harm than good. He's thinking that maybe he should have accepted this assignment on the condition that he speak only on his own area of experience and expertise.

The fifth principle of CVA is to always be sensitive to the needs of your audience. A well-known lecturer and author of business books is asked to give a keynote speech to a manufacturers' convention in Miami on the ongoing threat to the nation's economy after the 9/11 terrorist attacks. To the surprise of the conventioneers, the author speaks for 45 minutes on what he calls the panglobal "übermarket" and China's rapid emergence as America's number one economic challenge. He's good, and the subject is interesting, but not five minutes into his spiel, the audience is wondering if they might be in the wrong room. Actually, they're in the right room. A woman whispers to the person sitting next to her that she heard this guy give the same routine to a distributors' convention just a few months earlier.

Later, it turns out that the author simply ignored the assignment—even though he had written a well-received article in *The New Yorker* on the subject of terrorism and the economy and had appeared on CNBC talking about it. The word starts going around that he gives the same speech to every audience at about $30,000 a pop. In the end, while China's growth is a valid topic, it is not what the manufacturers had come to hear, and they aren't happy. The story gets out and adversely affects the author's speaking income for more than a year.

The sixth principle of CVA is to speak in pictures. A senior partner in a giant consulting company accepts an invitation to talk to pharmaceutical industry executives about government controls. He shows up with a laptop that turns out to be chock full of scores of fiendishly complex charts and tables that cruise across the screen too quickly to be deciphered or even comprehended. That in itself is a bummer, and the pharm people don't appreciate it. But that's not the real problem. The real problem is that the consultant is talking in broad, consultantese abstractions, waxing eloquent about "algorithmic metrics," "inverse projections," "parabolic calibrations," "parameter-scaled indices," and all kinds of sophisticated-sounding blather that turns off just about everybody in the room. But the consultant is too caught up in his own self-importance to notice the thousand-yard stares. Meanwhile, the mystifying slides continue their relentless and mind-numbing march to nowhere.

If he could read their minds, the consultant would know that these people want the same information, but they want it translated into an interesting and digestible mental meal of word pictures, stories, and anecdotes. Instead of "algorithmic metrics," they want to hear war stories about how governmental intervention is destabilizing prices across Africa. Instead of "inverse projections" (and the swarms of data figures that goes with them), the pharm people want actual case studies of what happens to certain markets when promising pipeline drugs suddenly disappoint in clinical trials. Instead of "parabolic calibrations," they want solid brand-name evidence of the fiscal relationships between R&D shortfalls worldwide and predictable market cycles. Instead of "parameter-scaled indices," they want to hear about what they can expect when markets behave unexpectedly.

What they get, however, is an insensitive consultant trying to show them how smart he is, how hard he works, and how excruciatingly exhaustive his research has been. When the execs leave, they feel almost like they've been locked in a room with a professor teaching a course in a foreign language. The one thing they all agree on is that this person will not be asked back.

The seventh principle of CVA is preparation. In New York, an authority on environmental law is talking to 300 chemical engineers and decision makers from a big paint company. His presentation seems poorly prepared. He gets lost twice trying to navigate his own PowerPoint presentation. He has to stop and sift through his notes. He jumps from subject to subject with no apparent connection between one and the other. He incorrectly refers to competitors' products, unaware that these products are made by his host company. He talks in the present tense about the company's CEO, who actually left the firm two years earlier.

If he weren't so tangled in a web of his own making, he might notice the looks of open-mouthed dismay in his audience, a small army of disenchanted pilgrims who can scarcely believe what they are seeing.

CVA, as you can see, is a must for the articulate executive in action. Never bore. Give value. Rule your PowerPoint—don't let it rule you. Talk from experience. Know whom you're talking to. Tell stories. And be ready.

For the potential of vast riches that could lie at the end of your rainbow, is CVA too much to ask?

STEPPING ON THE GAS: ADDING POWER

A t the center of CVA lies a simple yet potent architecture that I introduced in my book, *The Articulate Executive—Learn to Look, Act, and Sound Like a Leader*. I call it the *POWER formula*. The POWER formula is all you will ever need to create the perfect business presentation time after time, year after year. I know, because thousands of people have e-mailed or written to tell me how POWER has positively changed their careers and even their lives.

The POWER formula has only five elements:

1. Strong start
2. One theme
3. Good examples to support the theme
4. Ordinary language
5. Strong ending

> **Those looking for career advancement owe it to themselves to engrave a snapshot of POWER in their minds.**

It's so easy, even a child can understand it—and yet business professionals everywhere operate without POWER their entire careers. And it shows. Unfortunately, we can ignore POWER only at our peril. Those looking for career advancement owe it to themselves to engrave a snapshot of POWER in their minds. Take a look at the schematic on the opposite page, and try to remember it.

Implementing POWER is simply a matter of casting off bad habits and embracing what works. Twenty-five years of executive coaching tell me that this transformation could be the singlemost important decision you will ever make in your working life. If you want a comprehensive understanding of POWER and how to use it to your immediate advantage, I suggest that you have a close look at POWER in *The Articulate Executive*.

For the moment, I simply want to make the point that the beating heart of CVA is POWER and that both are as accessible—and vital—as filling your car tank with gas (to further the analogy, to proceed without CVA and POWER is like putting diesel fuel into a gasoline engine).

Now let's see what happens when we apply a little CVA/POWER to an everyday business presentation. Do you remember your last presentation? If you don't routinely make presentations, do you remember the last time you saw or heard one you thought was a good one? What made it good? Chances are that if you thought it was good, you may not have known exactly why.

Now you do.

Suppose, for example, that you're the senior technology officer of a small company with a big potential high-tech breakthrough. But to make the break and go the next couple of steps to complete commercial development of this new technology, you need a cash infusion. Where do you get it? Do you get it from an initial public offering (for different

The POWER Formula

*P*unch
1. Personal story
2. Anecdote or illustration
3. Begin with the ending (strong statement)
4. Rhetorical question
5. Quotation
6. Project into future
7. Look into past
8. Humor (tell as if true, make business point, don't blow punch line, and be appropriate).

*O*ne theme
One message, one mission, one theme only. But you may discuss that one theme in may different ways.

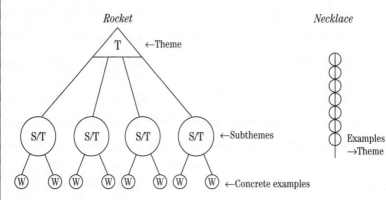

*W*indow
Specific examples, illustrations, and anecdotes to provide proof.
(This is how you let audiences actually see inside your presentation.)

*E*ar
Stay conversational. Don't "speechify."

*R*etention
1. Summarize key point or key points—one or three. One is best.
2. Loop back to beginning.
3. Ask audience to do something specific.
4. Project into future.
5. Bad news/good news.
6. Tell symbolic story that embraces your message.

reasons, the timing is wrong), from venture capitalists (maybe), or from another company that recognizes your potential blockbuster patent assets and research capabilities and has enough interest to at least listen to what you have to say? (A little heads-up research reveals that the "suitor" company is quietly in the market looking for the "next big thing.") Maybe they'll buy a piece of you or gobble you up in one big bite, and then you and everybody else with equity can go to the beach (maybe you can even reinvest and start a new company).

But right now you're burning cash. The original investors are skittish. They won't step up to the plate for the second round of financing, and you've got to do something fast.

You and your management decide to woo the company that's hovering in the wings. This could be your last chance. As a cofounder of the company, you draw the straw to make the critical presentation.

What would you do?

If you're like most people, you might clutch. You're thinking, what should I say? Then with a silent groan you suddenly realize that you could be sequestered from your job and other responsibilities for a solid month trying to put this "Fat Albert" together. You start imaging endless slides, an information-packed dissertation. You're thinking, If I don't hit them with all we've got, maybe they won't take us seriously.

The fact is that you hardly know where to begin.

After a few nights of staring at the bedroom ceiling, you finally decide to bite the bullet and try to get something on paper.

You write: "Good morning, I would like to thank you for coming. Before I begin this presentation, I would like to state that we are pleased to have this opportunity to interface with you and attempt to articulate the synergies that we believe accrue to both sides of this proposed merger. Now, I would like to outline the agenda for today's meeting. First, I will discuss the history of both our companies. Second, I will review our performance for the last 12 months. Third, I will give an in-depth overview of our technology development."

Let's stop there. This is just the beginning, but we're already heading for trouble. First, do we have a strong start? I think not. We have a conventional start that sounds not at all like a conversation but a lot like a presentation. We even use the word *presentation*, which is a signal that a predictable level of audience boredom is likely to follow.

Second, we're using words contrary to the way most of us normally speak (*state, interface, articulate, synergies,* etc.).

Third, we're speaking in the first person singular—*I*—when a consistent use of *we* would be more inclusive and appropriate.

Fourth, we're eating up valuable real estate giving an agenda when we could be capturing their minds with an anecdote, say, that quickly establishes a theme (besides, they can read the agenda in the handout or document).

Fifth, we have no theme.

Sixth, we're about to dive into the past (a history of both companies) when what they really want to hear about is the future. Besides, the last thing they need right now is a lecture on their own company—and if they've done even a token amount of homework or due diligence, they already know almost as much about the history of your company as you do.

Seventh, they already know your performance. That's why they've agreed to listen.

Eighth, an in-depth review of technology development is probably, in this case, more than they need to know for two reasons: (1) They already have a fundamental understanding of the technology and its commercial value (otherwise, they wouldn't be there), and (2) *in-depth* usually means an exhausting review of methodology and a history of technological development, which is probably inappropriate for this audience of senior management people.

So much for the conventional approach.

Now let's try a POWER start.

How about starting with the bottom line? But what is the bottom line?

The bottom line will always reveal our theme. (The theme is the best possible case you can make and will ultimately decide the fate of the deal.)

Every "presentation" you've done or ever will do has a theme—a message—that sums up the story behind the numbers and statistics.

Your company is in a tight race to produce the first plug-and-play device capable of unifying all the electronics and electronic devices in the ubiquitous "smart house" of the near future in one little hand-held remote.

This device will be easy enough for a child to use yet secure and powerful enough to operate up to a mile from your home.

Now instead of writing about how nice it is that we're all in this meeting, you're writing: "If we can find the money to finish research and development, we will bring to market the world's first unit capable of controlling every electronic device in every home in America . . . all in a three-ounce hand-held device no bigger than a cell phone . . . and costing less than a VCR.

"We already have a prototype and expect to have the product on store shelves by this time next year . . . at least six months in advance of our nearest competitor, incorporating Six Sigma quality and competitive pricing that could position us not only as first to market, but commanding the market for years to come."

It's all true. As good as it is, you know you're not promising too much. So now you've got both your strong start and your theme—and your CVA is starting to shape up as well.

I'll spare you the rest—but you can see where I'm going with this. You've laid out the hypothesis. Now you've got to provide the conclusion. You've got to back up everything you've promised and prove the case with well-chosen examples.

Here's where the numbers come in. You can talk about projections, analyze the competition, highlight proprietary technology breakthroughs, run through the business plan, throw up select financial slides, discuss risk, and show schematics. Most important, you can "speak in pictures"—give anecdotal evidence. It's all good because it all exists for one purpose only—to support the theme.

And don't forget—now you're talking conversationally. Instead of "synergistic," you're saying "one size only." Instead of "satellite sales configurations," you say "test market."

Before you know it, you've motored right through your conversation/presentation, and it's time to say something like, "It all comes down to this. . . ."

What it comes down to, as I said, is the story behind the numbers. So now you just go back and paraphrase what you said in the beginning.

And there it is—the perfect presentation. Punch. One theme. Windows (examples, proof). Ear (ordinary language). Retention (strong ending).

How did you do against the CVA checklist? Let's see:

	Yes	No
1. Did you bore?		✓
2. Did you add value?	✓	
3. Did you master your own presentation?	✓	
4. Did you talk about what you know?	✓	
5. Did you know your audience?	✓	
6. Did you talk in pictures?	✓	
7. Did you do your homework?	✓	

It sounds to me like your pistons are all firing. Now it's time to start lapping the competition.

LAPPING THE FIELD

We can talk about courage, integrity, character, refinement, resolve, dignity, and any number of other positive characteristics to try to define leadership and what makes a great leader. But what gives these characteristics life and muscle is *communications value added* (CVA). Without CVA, even the most qualified and promising of leaders may languish despite their undeniably admirable qualities and businesses drift without vision or purpose.

Gifted practitioners of CVA routinely exhibit many of what I might call the *hi-C's*: concept, conviction, clarity, candor, credibility, character, coolness, concentration, color, competence, crispness, civility, consistency, continuity, creativity, cohesion, caring and, of course, communication. As you saw in Chapter 2, GE's CEO Jeff Immelt incorporates most of these characteristics almost every time he has a chance to speak for his company.

By contrast to the hi-C's, people who lack CVA might share any mix of the following: emptiness, uncertainty, fuzziness, artifice, doubt, lack of character, fear, absentmindedness, drabness, incompetence, blather, boorishness, confusion, disjointedness, mediocrity, sloppiness, indifference, and alienation. If you are in a position of leadership and consistently demonstrate these negatives, the consequences both to you and your business could be harsh.

Anyone serious about his career should ponder those contrasts. Are you fuzzy, drab, indifferent, and alienated? Do you find yourself locked in mediocrity, surrounded by second- and third-rate performers? Can you do better? Do you want more? Read the list one more time, and think about it.

Concept. "We have only one purpose—we live to serve the demands and expectations of all our customers." (Sets the course.)

Emptiness. "We will continue to explore how to maximize profit." (Goes nowhere.)

Conviction. "We will overcome." (Resonates; Martin Luther King.)

Uncertainty. "There is nothing we can do." (Falls flat.)

Clarity. "In the third quarter we expect to expand further into insurance products, derivatives, private banking, and corporate finance." (Spells it out.)

Fuzziness. "We will continue our activities in financial services." (Tells us nothing.)

Candor. "We have made mistakes, and we have learned from our mistakes." (Honest.)

Artifice. "The business is in good hands. . . . we have no regrets and no issues." (Not so honest.)

Credibility. "We don't know all the answers, and we can do better." (Believable.)

Doubt. "We're the most talented, the biggest, the most powerful— nobody can touch us!" (Get serious.)

Character. "We promise to stand by our products, our customers, and our people." (Promises count.)

Lack of character. "We've got one year to double our profits. How we get there is your business." (Unwise guidance.)

Coolness. "The months ahead will not be easy, but we will get there one day at a time." (Level-headed and steady.)

Fear. "Your job is at stake. . . . the company is on the verge of collapse. . . . the competition is ruthless. . . . we are operating from weakness." (One foot already in the grave.)

Concentration. "We have a three-year plan, a working budget, and some of the best people in the business. Now here's exactly what we've got to do—and how we're going to do it." (Focus.)

Absentmindedness. "We will continue to discuss possible options in terms of devising a strategy to meet challenges." (Wishy-washy.)

Color. "Pick up your feet . . . put a little dance in your step . . . clap your hands . . . do whatever it takes to pump a little extra energy into your work. . . . We're all at our best when we're having fun." (Lively language.)

Drabness. "In terms of productivity, it has been shown that task repetition and stress can create attitudinal negativity that is contrary to the proper fulfillment of our assigned responsibilities." (Snooze.)

Competence. "Big changes are sweeping our industry. And that's good because change presents opportunity. But our customers expect us to deliver the same kind of competency, character, and ethics that have always set us apart in the past . . . and which I know you will deliver in the future." (Wisdom.)

Incompetence. "With the market worsening, we are taking steps to cut costs. First, I would like to announce that we are eliminating the Christmas party this year." (Dopiness.)

Crispness. "The best people. Hard work. A passion for innovation. Consistent results. Customer care. Flexibility. And a real desire to always meet change with constant improvement. That's what this company is all about." (Voice of leadership; Jeff Immelt.)

Blather. "We must implement protocols in terms of attempting to prioritize strategies favorable to long-term strategy going forward." (Voice of the bureaucrat.)

Civility. "Our competition is skilled, enterprising, and always looking for ways to take market share. . . . they are worthy of our attention and a daily reminder of why we can take nothing for granted." (Dignity.)

Boorishness. "We are the biggest and boldest, and we are going to kick some serious butt." (Buffoonery.)

Cohesion. "Our challenge comes down to just one thing: We will always try to act before we are forced to react." (Focus.)

Sloppiness. "We've been kind of busy, so we haven't really thought things through yet . . . but we'll get to it and then maybe we'll have some idea where we're going, and we'll try to let you know." (Say what?)

Consistency. "We have obstacles ahead, but if there's one thing I want you to remember from today, it's the same thing I've been trying to hammer home for the past six months: Stick with the plan! Stick with the plan! Stick with the plan!" (Reinforcement.)

Confusing. "We face challenges that require legislature and legal oversight. Therefore, our options are limited and our future unclear. . . . so I am unable to say what—if anything—we are going to do." (Cluelessness.)

Continuity. "In 2000 we acquired a company to strengthen our medical imaging business. . . . In 2001 we established a market presence in China and India. . . . Last year we invested over $1 billion in research and development. . . . And this year we will build a brand-new wind power business from scratch. . . . All this adds up to growth." (Big picture.)

Creativity. "We are at a crossroads. From now on we do more with less, and we do it through the magic of innovation. Nothing is more exciting than innovation—innovation in product development, innovation in how we run our businesses, innovation in how we market and sell our products and services, and innovation in how we deliver value to customers and investors." (Vision.)

Mediocrity. "We will continue to monitor costs vigorously, which will necessitate a discontinuation of all new product development, marketing, indefinite postponement of expansion of customer service centers, output reduction, and a head count reduction of 8 percent across the board." (Lack of vision.)

The articulate executive in action will favor the hi-C's every time.

THE 50 PERCENT SOLUTION: FILLING THE POTHOLES IN YOUR CAREER PATH

Business schools bemoan the fact that their students are quant savvy but unable to express themselves, and corporations privately complain that some of their smartest people are ineffective communicators.

This is what I call the *50 percent problem*. The 50 percent problem says that if you're not competent with language, you're not likely to connect, no matter how smart you are, and that such a liability will have a negative impact on your business. The answer to the 50 percent problem is the *50 percent solution*. The 50 percent solution says that if you can begin to look, act, and sound like a leader in all your communications, your career will flower, and your business will bear fruit.

A once-shy client told me about his time in the service as a junior aide to an admiral. When the young officer's stint was up, the admiral took him aside and offered words of wisdom. "You do a nice job, son," the admiral said. "I can count on you to follow orders and follow up. You've got a good head for solving problems, and I like how you worry about the details. But I'm going to offer just one piece of advice. . . . If you're going to get ahead, whether it's the military or the private sector, you're going to have to learn to speak in front of groups."

"That was the best advice I ever got," my client told me. He enrolled immediately in a Dale Carnegie course and got an entry-level job in the management training program of a regional bank. Twenty-three years later he was president and CEO.

"The Dale Carnegie course showed me I was meeting only part of my potential," he said. "Once I got comfortable on my feet and in meetings, it just seemed like my career started to take off."

Would things have gone differently had he not heeded the admiral's advice? "I'm certain I wouldn't be where I am today," he told me. "I see that bit of timely advice from the admiral as the turning point in my career."

A onetime administrative assistant found herself in a bad spot. She was smarter than her boss, full of energy and ideas, and eager to move up to something more challenging. But she kept hitting her head on a glass ceiling. She was thinking about quitting and taking her talents elsewhere when one day she got an assignment to help organize her company's annual conference of senior corporate officers in another city.

Unleashed from the daily routine, she jumped in with both feet. Coworkers quickly recognized her considerable organization skills, and before long, she found herself in charge of the whole project. Part of the new job required biweekly reports to the management committee. Her confidence and obvious enthusiasm, as well as her emerging management skills, quickly got the attention of the top people.

The conference went off without a hitch. In fact, it went so well that the company created a new position, events manager, that reported directly to a member of the management committee, the senior vice president of marketing. In this case, the 50 percent problem prevailed right up until she was moved out of her dead-end job. The 50 percent solution kicked in the first time she sat down at a conference table to report to senior management.

"Here's the problem," she said in that first meeting. "We've spent over $3 million already for promotions and sponsorships to support the brand, but it turns out that the advertising and marketing people we hired two years ago to run focus groups aren't talking to the right people or asking the right questions. I know because I sat in on two meetings this week."

"First of all, they're talking to adults, but it turns out that with the development of more recent software, demographics have shifted to tech-savvy teens and preteens."

"Second, the focus people are asking customers if they like it but not *why* they like it—and it turns out that kids are trying the product not because it's fun and informative but because it helps them with their homework. The buzz is big with this product right now, and we almost missed it."

The result: A rapid ramp-up in production to meet demand and a complete revamp of the events marketing campaign to appeal to the new audience, leading to brand extensions, a tripling of profits in just one year, a category leader in the industry, and an overnight success story.

Within two years, she was promoted yet again to vice president, brands. The company's signature brand revived. Market share doubled. Headhunters came calling, and today she is CEO of a $550 million consumer products company.

"She knew her stuff," the marketing chief told me later. "She had confidence and spoke well. She was crisp in the meetings, very articulate, and had no problems with the Q&A. . . . We were sorry to see her go."

The 50 percent solution ignites whenever you decide to put a match to it. The only requirements are a willingness to look beyond your current circumstances and the determination to press your case until you finally win what you want. This may require a conversation, presentation, declaration, meeting, negotiation, or sale—plus a singlemindedness you might have thought yourself incapable of. For all the frustrations and setbacks you might expect, the payoff is undeniably worth it, as the following examples show:

- The salaried worker at a manufacturer who does not hesitate to offer suggestions on improving shop floor productivity and winds up shop foreman.
- The biology researcher who gets over her fear of presenting papers at scientific conferences and suddenly finds herself a category expert on the Science Channel and ultimately the CEO of her own research firm outside Boston.
- The recent hire at an investment bank who sees an opportunity no one else even imagined in new financial instruments, successfully lobbies his management, generates hundreds of millions of dollars, gets promoted to managing director, and ends up running a separate profit center within the bank before age 30.
- The once-shy software programmer who sets out on an exhausting personal quest to sell his proprietary operating platform door to door and coast to coast until a private equity investor finally bites for $2 million, allowing the programmer to start his own firm, which he eventually sells to Microsoft for $160 million.
- The maverick-minded analyst at a boutique risk-management firm who sees pending disaster in the arrival of a new but inexperienced management team and organizes his fellow analysts into a power bloc that bolts the shaky enterprise en masse, sets up a competing business that overwhelms the bumbling tyros at their old firm, and establishes what grows to become a powerhouse in the industry.

None of these success stories would have become reality had not someone decided to stand up, speak up, and make something happen. These innovators are successful because they kept an eye out for opportunity—always looking to improve, grow, widen, or expand—and when they saw it, they never blinked.

In other words, they all operated on high-octane CVA, grabbed the 50 percent solution, and ran with it.

The CEO of a Fortune 10 company recently told me the qualities he looks for in a senior officer are "poise," "grace under pressure," "a talent for numbers," "brains," "comfortable with groups of any size," and "good with people."

He might as well have been talking about himself. And I have no doubt that if he were to step down tomorrow, so would the market value of his company.

THE RACE

CHAPTER

7

FIRST, GO FOR THE GUT

I often talk about what I call *primal mind*. Primal mind doesn't listen to data, argument, or appeal. We may have decent numbers for the long term, but primal mind is only thinking quick results. We may think we've built a case, but he's already made up his mind. We may want to talk about the marketing plan, but he wants to hear only what's in it for him. We may be deep into a review of performance to date, but he's day-dreaming about the new intern. He's not such a great guy, you're thinking, but let's face it, he is often *us*. We are all primal mind. It's only human nature. And if we're going to tap into the open wire between any two minds, we've got to get to know this beast.

Primal mind is always visceral, never cerebral. Primal mind reacts to the gut. Primal mind senses things, vaulting over the oblivious conscious mind to pick up vital clues governing our greatest hopes and fears, loves and hates. Primal mind isn't interested in our intellectual aplomb. It doesn't care if we're smart or even if we're dumb.

49

Primal mind kicks the tire and decides to buy the car. It steps through the door and says, "This is it" and decides to buy the new house. It shakes the hand and knows right then and there that this is the right person for the new job.

As I said in *The Articulate Executive*, this is the guy who makes all the important decisions and runs our lives.

That is why this is the guy we really want to be talking to.

> **What they need to hear is what it takes to make something happen.**

On this score, businesspeople can take a lesson from history. For millennia, historical leaders have gone straight for primal mind, bypassing the rational almost completely. Why? Because if you want to get something done well and quickly and you want everybody lined up behind the cause, talking only to the intellect can be a waste of time. We don't have to be orators or Svengalis, but we are always closest to our inner leader when our gut reveals what our audiences need to hear. What they need to hear is what it takes to make something happen. Listen, for instance, to Queen Elizabeth I, Henry VIII's only surviving child. She's preparing to address her troops, riding on horseback to the head of the army as the Spanish Armada approaches England in 1588. Philip II of Spain, one of Elizabeth's spurned suitors, has sent the "invincible" fleet against Protestant England. The future of the country hangs in the balance.

Elizabeth pulls herself up high in her saddle and speaks.

"My loving people!" she shouts. "Let tyrants fear"!

In a language of another age, she prepares to lead her army in battle. "I am come among you at this time . . . to live or die . . . to lay down, for my God and for my Kingdom and for my people, my honor and my blood."

Eyes blazing, she cries out: "I know I have the body of a weak and feeble woman. But I have the heart of a king!" She proudly defies the King of Spain and then vows "a famous victory over the enemies of my God, of my Kingdom, and of my people."

As it happens, the armada runs into a nasty storm and winds up mostly wrecked on rocks. But if you believe contemporary chroniclers, maybe it was kind of a blessing in disguise, a lesser of two evils—for the Spanish.

Accounts tell how the queen's passionate call to arms drove her well-armed soldiers nearly crazy with blood lust and a wild urge to slaughter the invaders. For Philip's people, it definitely would not have been a good day at the beach—thanks largely to the CVA of a 118-pound redhead.

In 1775, Patrick Henry rose to speak to a church filled with colonial delegates. Bursting with revolutionary zeal, he roared: "Suffer yourselves not to be betrayed by a kiss. . . . Are fleets and armies necessary to a work of love and reconciliation? . . . Is life so dear, or peace so sweet, as to be purchased at the price of chains and slavery? . . . I know not what course others may take—but as for me, give me liberty or give me death!"

That's early American CVA.

I'm not suggesting that you try to express yourself with this kind of heightened drama. You'd sound pretty silly if you tried. But a straight call to action from a great business leader or coach can have the same galvanizing effect. A sense of purpose, direction, and confidence ignited by an inspired leader can accomplish almost any objective.

Just one example is fabled Green Bay Packers' head coach Vince Lombardi, who is remembered not so much for leading his team to two consecutive Super Bowls but for single-handedly lifting an entire organization of mediocre performers to a level of brilliance that they never dreamed they could achieve.

Throughout history, muscular language has always had more impact than the abstract. Few people understood the power of words better than another wartime leader, Winston Churchill, who seized on the radio as the weapon of widest opportunity to marshal England against the Nazis. Had he not, many historians believe that people would be speaking German in Trafalgar Square today.

We need not be a Vince Lombardi, Winston Churchill, Queen Elizabeth, or Patrick Henry, but business without CVA is like a glass half empty. If business leaders today have vision, conviction, or passion, they rarely show it. The truth is that the leader *is* the message. The leader *is* the company. So is the telephone operator, the receptionist, the customer service rep, the field engineer, the district sales manager, and even the guy who delivers product to the bay behind the customer's store. If all these people can be led to the well, and if they can be inspired to drink of the vision, the conviction, and the passion, then they can all speak in one voice. They can all promote the party line.

One of my clients, a senior manager at Mercedes-Benz USA, never realized his true voice until after he had concluded an interview with a TV crew covering a humdrum local business story. With the camera still rolling, the newswoman suddenly said something about how much fun it must be to work for Mercedes-Benz. In an instant, the executive brightened and loosened up. Then he was off and running, unaware the camera was still on, about all the things he loved about his company and his job. The dour business stiff was gone and in his place was an entirely different person. This person was a man on a mission.

The newswoman was so impressed, she showed the videotape to the astonished manager—contrasting his droning, flat, official "executive" on-air personality with the robust and animated stranger who appeared on the accidental postinterview tape segment. Not only did the newswoman replay the tape, she actually recast the interview and repositioned the story to use portions of the "off camera" segment.

> *On-camera language:* "It is imperative to reposition strategic directives in order to implement entry-level marketing efforts."
> *Straight talk:* "We're trying hard to appeal to the 23 million twenty-somethings looking to buy their first affordable luxury car."
> *On-camera language:* "Our engineering expertise, quality of design and manufacture, and customer loyalty are unparalleled."

Straight talk: "My kids tell me the C series is the coolest car they've ever seen. . . . And I can tell you from personal experience this car is not only cool, but a dream to drive. . . . It's priced like a Ford but handles like a Ferrari."

On-camera language: "Female demographics indicate a potentially significant correction in purchasing patterns from vans and SUVs toward hybrid vehicles and sportier models."

Straight talk: "We're now starting to see among women what we saw a few years ago with men—a big shift from the practical to the sporty."

This experience was an epiphany for the executive, who for the first time understood the true value of his own CVA. For the first time he saw the business value in simply allowing himself to be himself. Thereafter, he actively sought opportunities to tell the Mercedes story in the media. The payoff, he says, was favorable press at a time when Mercedes needed it the most.

As was the case with my Mercedes client, primal mind, like a genie, is always looking for an opportunity to bust out of the box we've locked him in.

Sometimes primal mind is so smothered, we start gibbering in corporate "robo-speak," as in this example:

Inasmuch as we will endeavor to utilize our resources to implement a significantly lower cost structure heretofore lacking in our strategic plan, it is mandatory that every effort is exercised to redirect our priorities toward a heightened concern relative to topline growth.

Do you really talk this way? Does anybody really talk this way? Believe it or not, some people do.

But you shouldn't. Nor should you write this way. In fact, ideally, you should write the way you talk and talk the way you write (as I am trying to do in this book).

Like it or not, we are all judged by the way we talk. Our language, grammar, syntax, and choice of words reveal in large part who we are, where we come from, and our level of education, sophistication, and social status.

Many people believe that a more formal choice of words will endow them with a certain element or level of sophistication. Unhappily, this is most often not the case. In fact, the reverse is usually true (we'll leave Fed Chairman Alan Greenspan out of this because his highly formalized choice of words and ambiguous syntax are there for a reason and fully intentional).

In business, your choice of words shapes your career—negatively and positively.

The good news is that with words alone you have it within your power to create the person you want to be. No one will fault you for saying *implement* instead of *launch* or *nevertheless* instead of *yet* or *significantly lower* instead of *slash*. Sometimes a mix of formal and less formal is actually desirable, depending on circumstances. And in some cases, the more formal word may impart a more precise meaning and be the obvious choice. But in general usage, it is almost always preferable to favor the shorter, more Anglo-Saxon, more muscular words over their Latinized and more elaborate counterparts.

The examples are endless, but here's a sample list of what I'm talking about:

Weak Word	Power Word
reduce	cut
significantly lower	slash
maintain	keep
maintain	believe, think
effectuate	spur
nevertheless	yet

Weak Word	Power Word
heretofore	to now
therefore	so
however	but
inasmuch as	since
acquire	buy, grab
margin	profit
alleviate	ease, relieve
donate	give
delete	strike
manufacture	make
appeal	ask
significant	big
insignificant	very small
indicate	show, reveal
indicator	sign
derive	get
venture	thrust
fashionable	hot
unfashionable	passé, uncool
large sector	big chunk
deliberate	argue
vastly overwhelm	crush
implement	launch
predicate	base
retract	take back
estimate, postulate	guess
extemporaneous	off the cuff
application	use (noun)
utilize	use (verb)
elementary	basic
endeavor	try

Again, I'm not saying that shorter words are always necessarily better. But given a clear choice, I would go with the shorter because the shorter is more conversational and vigorous. As an example, here are a few brief makeovers of the convoluted paragraph we began with:

We've got to cut costs, and we will. [CEO to the troops.]

Costs are now a big issue, and we should be doing everything we can to save money. [CFO to CEO.]

The message is: We're spending too much money in this department. . . . I've got a plan to help us cut costs. [Department head to managers.]

So we want to make sure we keep in mind that we're talking to people, not droidlike operatives or managerial machines. People who think, act, feel, and respond much like you do. People who have a heart as well as a mind. So reach for the heart as well as the head. Be yourself. Step on the gas. Talk to primal mind and see what happens.

FAST STARTS AND SMART CHARTS

A former associate of mine who used to be a presidential speech writer tells the story of the first time, as a young White House intern, he met President Nixon. The president listened impatiently, tapping his fingers on the Oval Office desk, as the intern took too long to get to his point. Finally, the president cut him off.

"What's the bottom line?" Nixon barked suddenly, interrupting the startled intern in midsentence. "What's your point?"

It was a lesson the young man never forgot. From that day, he always made it his business to dive straight to the bottom line. Years later, when he was writing speeches, he made sure the audience never had to wait long to get the message.

This should be the golden rule of business communications, and it should also run in reverse. If we are reporting up within our organization, we have the

> No senior person wants to wait to hear your point.

57

same responsibility to the leader as the leader has to us. In other words, each side is beholden to the other to tell the story with dispatch. No senior person wants to wait to hear your point. And no junior person should be forced to wait.

So before you have any business contact, it pays to chart your course wisely.

One of my clients complained that the meetings in his organization were taking up too much time and getting too little done. When I sat in on a couple of these meetings, I could see why. First, it was taking 40 minutes to deliver information that could have been delivered in just two. Second, several of these meetings had important messages that were buried under a blizzard of information. Third, most of that information was unnecessary. The data could have been better handled with a hard-copy handout (after a two-minute presentation), a selective use of pertinent numbers, and a longer question and answer period.

Information by itself is no more useful than a collection of facts. The manager who reports periodically to the management committee adds value by translating facts into information that's useful.

Someone asked, What's the difference between information and communication? The difference is that information is the delivery of data; communication is the delivery of knowledge. Communication is connection. Connection means action. Right action means profits. That's why the first obligation to any business audience is to *translate* complex information into a simple message delivered in ordinary language.

> **Information by itself is no more useful than a collection of facts.**

Let's say, for example, you're a brand manager for a midsize manufacturer of digital game products. You're reporting to your senior management team on the last quarter. You're expected to give the facts, and you could do just that—give the facts. Or you could choose to give the news (changes and developments) that the facts reveal, kind of a *translation* of data into a message.

If you just wanted to give the data, you might show a bunch of graphs and tables on a PowerPoint presentation. You'd walk your audience through what they had come to expect, a detailed review of the numbers: volume, market share, sales, projections, and so on, always in the same order. This approach might require 45 or 50 slides and almost an hour of management's time.

The alternative approach would require four or five slides and about 20 minutes. Here's how that would work: Your opening statement would be short, maybe 15 seconds, and it would tell the whole story. For instance, "On the whole, the news is good. We're seeing two new developments: an unexpected high demand for advanced graphic games in multiuse cell phones and expansion of commercial Internet use, where we already have a footprint. The only immediate negative issue is a 2 percent increase in product piracy, mostly Chinese knock-offs, and we're scheduled to meet with the State Department again on that."

Then you'd explain how you came to those conclusions, showing just a handful of graphs to prove the point. You'd wrap it up with a brief recap and go to Q&A.

Elapsed time: 18 minutes. One-third as long as you might have gone but three times as effective. That's why I tell clients that in a business environment, your best bet is always to begin with your ending. Start with the bottom line. In that way, if you are interrupted or run out of time, you're still covered. The information is already on the table.

And it's not a bad idea—just in case—to try to tell the *entire* story in the first few minutes (before you even show your first slide). This is the hallmark of a real pro who knows how to play the game. Step one: Present the case (no slides). Step two: Prove the case (slides). Step three: Lose the slides and paraphrase the point you made at the top. We'll have more to say about this in Chapter 21.

I also advise clients that sometimes it's better to begin with the future than with the past. Let's say, for example, that you're reporting up to senior management on the results of the last quarter. Chances are the senior team already has a pretty good idea of what those results are, so why not give them what they really want to know: How will these results affect the balance of the year for the business, or the next 18 months, or the next two years? Wouldn't it be more productive to reverse the process—begin with what you see coming (based on what you have gleaned from the last quarter's results)?

For example: "The next 10 months will be decisive. The market for handset games is expected to double before June 1. We still have a technology edge through our Indian and Korean partnerships, but we expect new competitors will begin flooding the market by the end of the summer. But if we can launch the new 7 series before July, our projections tell us we should be able to stay out ahead of the pack for at least another two years."

Then use what they were expecting—the numbers from the last three months—to explain how you came to your conclusions.

No need to tell your bosses what to do. Rather, simply give your interpretation of the changes and conditions you see in the data and suggest options for courses of action you think make sense (no doubt you will have some). This is how you provide added value and make yourself really useful (not to mention enhance your chances for advancement).

By looking out into the future, you automatically accomplish five objectives:

1. Relieve your bosses and peers of having to interpret all the data and information themselves.
2. Provide insights and ideas that add value.
3. Position yourself as a forward-looking person (top management prizes forward-looking people, who are often tapped for leadership positions).

4. Establish yourself as more of a peer than a functionary.
5. Gain a reputation as a high potential who can be counted on to be crisp, concise, and always have something interesting to say.

So give your career a jump-start. Impress your boss and the boss's boss. Start with the bottom line and project into the future. And while you're at it, try to tell the whole story right up front.

CHAPTER

9

HOW LEADERS DRIVE
THE MESSAGE

A mazing but true: A surprising number of CEOs are "so absorbed in what they want their company to be," according to one survey, that they never bother to tell their workers.

Can it be any surprise that after four years these CEOs often have little to show for their "vision"?

We all know where that vision's been hiding. It's hanging on the wall gathering dust up in the boardroom, where the CEO put it and nobody ever sees it. And it probably sounds a lot like a thousand other visions hanging unread and forgotten in a thousand other boardrooms all over America.

The short version of one such "vision" might be a pledge to "dominate the children's apparel market." But as Timothy Finley, CEO of Jos. A. Bank Clothiers, Inc., likes to point out: "The average run-of-the-mill Joe could care less if the boss's vision is to dominate the children's apparel market, or any market. . . . in the real world people don't think ahead more than six to eight months. . . . all they want is their paychecks and fair treatment."

Mr. Finley has a point and probably gets what he expects. But what if he were to expect—demand—more? What if he made everyone feel they had a personal stake in their work? What if they felt they were part of something bigger than a paycheck?

What if? What if Vince Lombardi hadn't been the Packers' coach?

Take Gordon Bethune, the onetime CEO of Continental Airlines, who almost single-handedly wrestled Continental out of a near-fatal tailspin. Bethune knows how to get things done, which means he knows how to lead. And it didn't happen by hanging around the executive floor and admiring the "vision" on the boardroom wall.

Bethune is a self-confessed glutton for action who drives a motorcycle and used to take personal delivery of new Boeing aircraft, flying them to Continental's Houston headquarters himself.

Bethune's style was one-third inspiration, one-third perspiration, and one-third motivation. To inspire workers, he launched a monthly bonus for placing in the top five in on-time rankings. Then he started shooting for the top three (extra bonuses) and set up a budget target incentive plan for the top 20 executives.

But Bethune didn't let memos or e-mail do his talking for him. He got right down on the floor with mechanics and flight attendants, pressing the flesh, sharing ideas, discussing strategy, telling people why he was doing what he was doing (people need to know that which affects their lives), and eliciting support.

He got it, and the results spoke for themselves.

Bethune's effect on Continental was like mounting a jet engine on a pickup truck. When the jet kicks in, instead of cruising the freeway, you're riding a rocket sled.

People like Gordon Bethune don't come along every day. In fact, what you're more likely to find at the top of any given organization is a well-meaning man or woman so unwittingly imbedded in the 50 percent problem (see Chapter 6) that growth and revenue opportunities pass them by every day.

Few Americans have ever heard of Konosuke Matsushita. But Matsushita was a real visionary generations ahead of his time who built a simple idea into a company we today call Panasonic. Way back in the 1930s, Matsushita was inspired by a visit to a Japanese temple complex where he was surprised to find people happily working for no money. The eye-opening lesson he gleaned from that experience was that if people feel they are performing meaningful work, they will be happier and more productive.

It was an epiphany for Matsushita, who began to preach a new gospel to his troops, one pithy aphorism after another.

- Treat people you do business with as if they were family.
- Service, not the sale, creates permanent customers.
- Being conscientious on the job is not enough. Rather, think of yourself as completely in charge of your job, and take responsibility for your work.
- If you can't make a profit with society's money, people, and resources, you are committing a crime against society.

In a day when corporate leaders in general and Japanese corporate leaders in particular rarely gave middle-level officers or the rank and file the time of day, Matsushita was like Moses preaching in the wilderness. Even by today's standards, his vision may have been a little ambitious, but his legend lives on at Panasonic, where workers still sing the company anthem and recite Matsushita's business principles.

It's interesting to speculate what the outcome might have been for the Matsushita corporation, and later Panasonic, had not Matsushita taken it on himself to articulate his vision. Like many a great leader, he was never so absorbed in what he wanted his company to be that he never bothered to tell his people.

That's CVA.

When Lou Gerstner took over as the new chief of IBM, he saw what had to be done—and made sure everybody knew it. Gerstner inherited a bloated bureaucracy that was beginning to function like a government. His course of action was clear: Swing the dial from manufacturing to service, cut waste, and start running IBM's many businesses—and IBM itself—as if each were an entrepreneurial enterprise.

Gerstner made sure everybody got the message—employees, customers, shareholders, Wall Street, even the man on the street. He used every opportunity he could find to spread the word: trade shows, annual meetings, TV interviews, and regular visits to IBM facilities all over the world.

By the time Gerstner retired in March, 2002, IBM was a different company because of his passionate pursuit of the party line, which had the effect of bringing a great lumbering beast back from the brink of death and then some. His memoir, *Who Says Elephants Can't Dance?* says it all.

When Ed Zander took over as CEO of Motorola, he found himself at the helm of a company that had lost its sense of direction. Like Xerox, Motorola was a onetime technology leader that stood by as competitors did a better job of commercializing Motorola's innovations. Zander looked around and saw that Motorola was doing too many things and not enough of them particularly well. Nor was Motorola capitalizing on its own strengths. He also saw that he had landed in the heart of a hidebound culture that couldn't get out of its own way.

Zander lost no time getting out of corporate headquarters to press the flesh, meet face to face with customers and employees all over the world, and try to figure out where the company ought to go. He did more listening than talking and came home with a game plan: Pare down the product line but beef up commitment to four markets—the individual, home, auto, and large organization. At the same time, he saw the need to concentrate efforts aimed toward "seamless mobility"—advanced technology that will let users transfer voice and data between offices, home, and car.

Customers were clear about what they wanted. The vision could wait.

> The great presentation always sounds more like a conversation.

"The world wants me to come up with this grand vision," Zander told *Fortune*, "but what I'm hearing from customers right now is 'execute.'"

But for execution to become a reality, Zander knew he would need to get all his people behind him. He made the rounds of employee meetings to lay out the rough plan and where he saw the company in five years. With execution starting to crank up, the vision began to fall in place.

"If seamless mobility is the big bet," he said, "then everybody in the company's got to get galvanized around it."

The giant began to stir. But Zander understood that a company embedded in 75 years of stuffy tradition does not become a star gymnast overnight. He was impressed with the projects and gee-whiz technology, although the communications style of his own people drove him almost to a migraine. When scientists and senior managers arrived with their presentations, he got a taste of the kind of plodding cultural environment he was dealing with—hundreds of slides and thousands of words per slide. But Zander is a relaxed, energetic type of leader not given to formalities, so it was only a matter of time before the scientists and managers began to loosen up a little themselves. The formal presentations started looking and sounding more like conversations. That made it easier to move fast, make decisions, and get more done.

Motorola is a work in progress, and the results will speak for themselves. But Ed Zander realizes he's got to keep listening, motivating, talking constantly to customers and employees, pressing the flesh across the globe, and lighting fires every day if Motorola is going to climb out of the muck and get back on track as a world leader in communications technology.

Steel-fisted Merrill Lynch CEO Stan O'Neal slashed costs with grim resolve, hacking 24,000 employees from the payroll, shutting 300 offices, and making himself one of the least-loved CEOs in Wall Street history. It didn't take him long to generate a reputation as an icy and distant bean-counting bureaucrat out to make a name for himself at the expense of his own people.

But Merrill employees counted themselves lucky a couple of years later when O'Neal's draconian measures started to pay off, and the newly lean, reorganized firm began posting record earnings—surpassing even those of the fat and happy late 1990s.

O'Neal thinks of himself as a man of action, not words. Still, his message, as he articulated it to his senior managers, trickled down through the ranks. The message couldn't be any clearer: *Merrill is changing fast from an old boys' club to a meritocracy*. This is not comforting news to what remains of the old guard, but it's music to the ears of the hardworking generation on its way up.

In an infrequent speech to Merrill employees, O'Neal takes the opportunity to explain that painful cost cutting is necessary. Numbers, he says, are more than numbers. Each individual number tells a story about what Merrill can be. The period of pain yields results, he says, that not only bring the company back from the brink but also deliver good news to investors, make stock buyback possible, and give Merrill the muscle to make acquisitions.

He's telling them that their sacrifices mean that Merrill can prosper in an industry becoming more competitive almost every day.

The effect is the beginning of a transformation. O'Neal's message softens their perception of him as a remote tyrant. People now see that he cares. In their minds he's more approachable. The fact that he's talking at all about a subject that affects them all is encouraging. There's now a sense that Merrill people are part of a new enterprise full of promise.

Now people get behind the message and the man. The payoff is a jump in profit margin from 17 percent to almost 30 percent in just two years.

Sam Walton built Wal-Mart on the principle of constant improvement, an abiding faith in the power of ordinary people, and a belief that one-stop shopping on a massive scale and rock-bottom prices were a sure-fire formula for success.

By the time Walton died in 1992, Wal-Mart—founded in 1962—had delighted investors and blown away its competition, including now-bankrupt K-Mart and Korvettes. Today Wal-Mart continues to grow worldwide.

Sam Walton's successor, David Glass, kept the ball rolling until he turned the reins over to the next CEO, Lee Scott.

In a *Fortune* interview, Glass, who joined the company in 1976 and still sits on the board, talked about what made Wal-Mart special right from the beginning.

"Sam had the desire to improve that I've not seen," he recalled. "I can count on one hand the people I've known who got up every morning and really tried to improve something—either in their business or in their daily lives."

"Sam felt we were all partners, and he shared financial information with everyone in every store. He believed that everyone should be an entrepreneur, . . . and we had grass roots meetings in every store. And there was an absolute belief that the best ideas ever at Wal-Mart came from the bottom up. . . . the door greeter, for example, was the idea of an hourly associate in Louisiana."

The heart of Wal-Mart's phenomenal success lies in its involvement of its own people in the process of constant improvement and an early commitment to technology, Glass said. On top of that was the belief that "nothing very constructive happens in the office. . . . We decided to send everybody out from . . . [headquarters] to the stores Monday through Thursday and bring them back Thursday night. On Friday morning we'd have our merchandise meetings. But on Saturday morning we'd have the sales for the week, and we'd have all the other information from [our] people who'd been out in the field, telling us what the competition was doing. So we decide then what corrective action we want to take. By noon on Saturday we had all our corrections in place. Our competition got their sales results on Monday. Now they're ten days behind, and we've already made the corrections."

Today Wal-Mart continues to barrel along under the twin banners of continuous improvement and employee involvement, growing almost by the week, setting benchmarks year after year, and leaving the competition in the dust.

When Jim McNerney took the top job at 3M, he walked into a company adrift, unable to boast a single commercial hit since Post-Its a quarter of a century earlier.

In addition to jump-starting 3M's legendary innovation machine, McNerney—a former GE superstar who lost the final bakeoff for the GE CEO position—took swift action across the board, including firing thousands of employees, focusing on health care and high tech, and setting rigorous performance measurements.

To his surprise, employees generally encouraged him to shake things up.

"I found a company who thought they weren't achieving all they could, and they were willing to team with somebody to do more," he told *BusinessWeek*.

So McNerney, a lifelong athlete and still an adult-league hockey player, became the head coach of the 3M company. First, he set high goals and demanded that his managers meet those goals. But he didn't just give orders and walk away. Instead, he began working with his team day in, day out, to help them make the grade.

Further down the ranks, McNerney is praised as an inspirational leader who is comfortable speaking to big groups or conversing one on one. Like any good coach, he's inclusive, passionate, constantly out in front of obstacles, and working daily toward the grail of excellence from all his players.

"My experience is that if people are convinced they're growing as they pursue company goals, that's when you get ignition," he said.

Finally, 3M had ignition. Within just two years of his arrival, profits and stock price were both up by more than a third.

McNerney's skillful practice of CVA could wind up adding hundreds of millions of dollars to 3M's bottom line.

It's true that Silicon Valley as we know it today was born in a California garage. But the digital age was not the child of two kids by the names of Gates and Jobs. Silicon Valley was actually born three decades earlier—in 1938—and the parents were two young men called Hewlett and Packard.

Both men understood from the start that their infant enterprise was only as good as their people. So they undertook a series of groundbreaking actions that would wind up being revolutionary not just in the provinces of high tech to come but also in the larger landscape of business itself.

Over the years, Hewlett and Packard launched innovations that today we take for granted. For example, they were among the first to

- Grant big bonuses to all employees when productivity went up
- Introduce profit-sharing plans
- Offer tuition assistance, job sharing, and flex time
- Eliminate office walls and doors by creating cubicles

Rejecting traditional corporate hierarchical structures and creating an egalitarian, a decentralized system opened the way for creativity and productivity gains already underway before the "official" high-tech revolution even began.

When Ed Haldeman took over as CEO of besieged Putnam Investments, the 67-year-old Boston firm was hemorrhaging cash as investors yanked their money—$3 billion a month—in the wake of trade scandals.

At the same time, he was startled to discover a cowboy culture layered with a rigid class hierarchy and mountains of petty, infuriating rules.

An industry veteran with a reputation as a straight arrow, Haldeman knew real change had to come, and fast. So he took up residence on the same floor as his portfolio managers—forgoing the luxurious twelfth-floor executive suite—and set to work trying to stem the cash outflow while relentlessly communicating his plans for organizational and cultural change.

He opened quarterly meetings to all employees. Rather than read speeches detailing highlights, he presided over free-wheeling sessions of give and take. He told everyone willing to listen of his plans to rein in the bureaucracy, appoint a new compliance chief, curtail short-term trading, and lower sales charges and other fees.

Within weeks, the nervous staff felt reassured enough to stop worrying and begin concentrating on running the business under the new guidelines. When he wasn't putting out fires in the office and calming fears among the staff, Haldeman was on the road working hard to reestablish relationships and set things right with rattled institutional investors.

"We explained to people what went wrong and what we're doing to fix it," he told *BusinessWeek*.

Putnam is a work in progress. But as Haldeman's longtime friend, Vanguard CEO John Bogle, says, "If anyone can do it, Ed can."

The message from all these stories is the same: If you've got something to say, make sure that your people aren't the last to know.

10

PUTTING THE TEAM IN
THE PASSING LANE

Business leaders routinely assemble managers and workers, tell them to "innovate," and then walk away—leaving employees shrugging their shoulders and scratching their heads.

CEOs say things like "We need to be an innovative company" in the annual report or in the statement. But being for innovation is like being for blue skies. Customers want new and improved. Better products. Better services. That's innovation.

Every business leader in the world is aware of the value of innovation, but few know how to make it a reality. The savvy executive understands that for innovation to become policy, several things have to happen.

First, get everybody excited.
Second, get them aligned.
Third, get out of the way.

When people are fired up and ready to go—or even if they're not—that's when Bryan Mattimore steps in. Bryan is a branding, creativity, and innovations expert and author of *99% Inspiration—Tips, Tales & Techniques for Liberating Your Business*.

Mattimore has found that sometimes what seems like the wackiest idea can produce the best results. Take the case of the two consumer products companies that merged. Predictably, the CEO of the combined companies gathers everybody together and says, in effect, "You've all got to start working as a team." Mattimore gets the call to make sure that happens.

But it's a sticky business. Neither side feels like a team, nor seems to want to. Suspicion and even hostility are everywhere. There's more of a sense of competition than cooperation. E-mails and voice mails go unanswered. Turf lines are being drawn, and people on both sides are quietly maneuvering to an advantage.

Paranoia is setting in, and both sides are so culturally and emotionally apart that productivity is plunging. It's a tough assignment by any measurement, but Mattimore has an idea.

You might expect him to launch a study of the situation and arrange for endless interviews with decision makers at all levels. Of course, you'd throw in your standard "in-depth analysis," an exhaustive written report of your analysis, a proposal for a course of action, a program of implementation, and maybe a kitchen sink. Then maybe some time next year you might be ready to implement.

In the world of consultancy as we know it, none of these things would seem unreasonable.

But instead, Mattimore has a party.

He gets everybody together and tells them to stop thinking about work and start making music. He teaches 200 people how to write songs and then tells them to start writing songs about their own brands. It sounds crazy, but before long, brand teams are huddling together creating songs. Then Mattimore starts holding dinners where teams get to perform their songs. The competition is fierce, but everybody is laughing and having a good time. There's a competition for the best Elvis and Mick Jagger impersonations, the best street music, the best lyrics, the best rock and roll, the best country, the best pop, the best blues.

By the time the last award is given and the zany musical adventure is over, there's not a trace of conflict or suspicion to be found. Everybody's relaxed now, on a first-name basis, the cultural barriers are down, the energy is up, the creative juices are cooking, and just about everybody feels pretty good about themselves, their jobs, and their new company. Best of all, nobody at the top has to read another "in-depth analysis." They don't have to read anything because the results are immediate and self-evident. Productivity comes roaring back, and revenues follow. Not surprisingly, this sudden reversal from clashing cultures to a single empowered team eventually gets the analysts' attention, and valuations start inching up as well.

> **Good executives have an ear for listening. Even if they know the answers, they ask questions.**

"It was nothing," Mattimore says later, feigning humility. "After all, we did it for a song."

That's the kind of music every CEO likes to hear.

Ultimately, the music of success should start in the corner office.

Good executives have an ear for listening. Even if they know the answers, they ask questions: "What do you think is the best approach?" "Do you think this idea makes sense?" "Are these the people we should be talking to?" "Do you see a better way?" "Have we left anything out?" Questions promote ownership of shared ideas, which, in turn, ratchets up performance through pride of participation. Questions build teamwork by unlocking talent and ideas. Questions make us all think harder and deeper. Questions help us learn.

While talented executives are questioning others, Mattimore is asking questions of executives. "Do you think this is the best idea you can come up with?" "Can you think of an even wilder concept?" "Have you thought about turning this around and looking at it through the eyes of an independent sales rep in Des Moines?"

In Mattimore's eyes, the gold standard of executive talent should always be measured through the barometer of creativity.

"The instinct to create is very strong in each of us," he says. "The trick is to help draw it out."

For example, in a "mindstorming" session with middle managers, Mattimore asked participants to write down as many ideas as they could think of—no matter how zany or bizarre—to try to come up with new ideas for home security alarm systems.

In a matter of minutes, the managers had produced not one or two but a half dozen ideas for new devices.

"The first five or so are usually old ideas," he says. "The next five are a little more interesting, more adventurous, but the next 10 after that are really new ideas."

To come up with original ice cream flavor names for an upscale market, Mattimore had a group of managers flip through a stack of magazines putting together images, words, and phrases in search of tantalizing combinations. A photograph of a symphony orchestra yielded "Raspberry Rhapsody." A comic book and *Popular Mechanics* produced "Cookie Dough Dynamo." Other images inspired "Midnight Brownie Crunch."

In the end, Mattimore's credo is a challenge for all leaders to improve performance—not just in branding and marketing but also in management, manufacturing, financial services—you name it—through creative thinking. And the best way to unleash creative thinking is to ask questions. Loosely translated (and with apologies to Bryan), the "Mattimore Manifesto" might go something like this:

1. If you don't ask, you don't get.
2. There's no such thing as a dumb question.
3. The question bag is never empty.

Any questions?

SPEED BUMPS:
A CAUTIONARY TALE

A predatory new CEO gets it into his head that he wants to cut costs. He wins the top spot at a culturally paternalistic offshore reinsurance company where morale is high, the workers feel like they're part of a big family, and the company's financial performance is consistently solid. Medical, compensation, and retirement benefits are outstanding. The gym is state of the art, the cafeteria foregoes Twinkies and cheese dogs in favor of healthy food, and there's even a nursery for babies and small children.

But the new CEO sees only bloat and waste. So the first thing he does is announce draconian cuts almost across the board and throughout the organization. The e-mail from the new CEO to department heads reads simply: "Effective immediately, you will reduce head count by 18 percent." Worse, whole departments are slashed. Benefits and amenities are cut. A pall of fear and panic falls over the entire organization. In a meeting, he tells the senior staff: "Either you're with me or against me. If you don't like it—there's the door. But you'll never work in this industry again." In the same meeting, he tells an off-color joke at the expense of women, ignoring the presence of two senior female executives in the room (both later quit). Morale sinks to rock bottom. In response to word of discontent throughout the ranks, he fires off another e-mail—this one in capital letters—which screams: "THERE IS NO ROOM IN THIS ORGANIZATION FOR WHINERS AND MALCONTENTS." People are so paralyzed worrying about their jobs that productivity drops to near zero in some departments.

It's well known that the new CEO is a workaholic who has virtually no other interests and routinely works 17-hour days. Naturally, he surrounds himself with like-minded widowmakers, part of the new entourage, who share more than a solid work ethic: They all parrot the views of the boss. There's not an independent thinker among them. So the CEO is safely insulated not only from the rest of his company but also from dissenting views or any creative, fresh thinker outside the official party orbit.

Firings and a flood of defections ensue. The word around the office is that while the CEO is firing people left and right—in some cases veteran employees close to retirement and their pensions—he's also using the company jet not only to travel on business (while the rest of the company is restricted to economy class on commercial flights) but also to take his family on a ski vacation to Aspen over Christmas.

To make matters even worse, it's now common knowledge that he had to axe 50 people in order to lock in his new management team with staggering pay and bonus packages.

Throughout, he neither seeks the counsel of respected veterans within the organization nor bothers to hold even a single meeting with middle managers.

One courageous manager, figuring she has nothing to lose, secures a 10-minute audience with the tsar in an attempt to warn him that the business is suffering. The new boss verbally assassinates the manager for her trouble. ("You think I'm stupid? I'll worry about the business—you better start worrying about keeping your job.")

Key people outside the inner circle and platoons of middle managers empty their offices and walk out. Chaos reigns for months. By the time things start to settle down, a number of important clients have also left. By the end of the fiscal year, productivity, market share, sales, and revenues are all heading south.

Thanks to some creative accounting, so are costs—at least on paper (don't forget those bonuses). But at the cost of what?

The point of this story is not that a new CEO cuts costs in an effort to save money and please the shareholders. Who can fault him for merely doing what any other tough-minded CEO would do? Never mind that he fires so many people that many will eventually have to be replaced (with irreparable loss of loyalty and talent). Never mind that he launches his frenzied slash and burn actually in a good economic cycle. Never mind that his long-term cost-cutting plan is more about costs than growth. And never mind that he can't see the potential power and productivity locked up inside each once-loyal professional in the firm.

The fact is that at some point way down the road the result of his chopping and slicing, even close to the bone, reasonably might be expected to bear some fruit.

No. The point of this story is that outside of a few terse, self-conscious, and graceless e-mails and memos, he never once bothers to articulate his vision to the people who most need to hear it—the worried workers down through the ranks. He never once bothers to explain why unpopular measures have to be taken for the greater long-term good of the firm. While he's in the office, he's only in *his* office. When he's not, he's on the company's Falcon jet.

About the same time, the new CEO at a competing offshore reinsurance company is taking similar measures to cut costs. But the results are strikingly different.

The new CEO at the competing firm does the same due diligence and comes to the conclusion that they probably can do more with less. He, too, launches a wave of cost cutting. But the effect is nowhere near so devastating, which means that the company never misses a beat in transition. And that means that while competitor number one is awash in ill will and confusion to the extent that business slows and falters, competitor number two is still making money, staunching defections, holding on to clients, and taking business away from number one.

When CEO number two talks about layoffs, he explains that these are largely due to redundancies from an earlier acquisition and couches the process of separation as a moment that could turn out to be—in many cases—a chance to even greater opportunity elsewhere (because in the United States and Britain small competing firms are starting up). He stresses that the severance pay is demonstrably generous, that special job counseling is available to all, and that the company is providing interim work space for anyone who wants to take advantage of it.

"And I would like to mention," he adds, "that neither I nor my senior team are exempt. We will all be taking a 20 percent cut in pay until this company returns to double-digit profitability."

When he talks about employees sharing a heavier burden for health insurance, he uses graphs and charts to show how skyrocketing insurance costs, if unchecked, "might actually start to threaten the financial strength of the company, which could in turn pose a new threat to jobs." While he's at it, he talks about his vision—how he expects to lead the company to number one or two in the next five years—and he lays out a road map so everybody can see how he plans to get there and how they can contribute individually and as a team to this worthy undertaking.

Overall, it's an inspiring message—in spite of the fact that the news is not all good—and they can all see it comes from the heart. They can see the passion. But they also can see he doesn't have to fake it. Importantly, they admire him, and they respect the fact that he delivers the news, both good and bad, in person and not facelessly via remote control. They respect the fact that he's taken the trouble to explain matters and tell the truth. They feel like they're listening to a coach, someone who can make sense of this challenging time of instability and bring them together. They're beginning to sense the excitement. They're beginning to believe that together they will achieve a common goal.

Of course, the perpetual naysayers and those left behind may have few kind words, but the rest of the company, the survivors, will feel their energy restored and their confidence renewed. They may be asked to work harder and longer, give up a few perks, but if the coach is good, he will make them all believers. He will make every individual feel important enough and empowered enough to exceed their own expectations. And if he's a smart coach, he will give his people enough latitude that they begin having fun and look forward to coming to work every day.

That's why company number two ends up eating company number one for lunch—and dinner, too.

12

FUEL INJECTION

Instead of paint, the creative businessperson works in strategies. Instead of clay or marble, he creates with numbers and ideas that translate into action. Where an architect might design an eye-popping church, the creative leader might design a brand-new company or engineer a brilliant merger or acquisition.

Articulation without a spark of creative inspiration behind it is like pizza without cheese. There's something missing—and audiences with a hunger for leadership and direction demand more. Cheese would be good, but extra cheese would be better.

Many credible people believe that while they may have some good ideas occasionally, creativity is not part of their package.

Wrong. Almost every person in every business meeting is not only credible but creative. The question is, To what degree? How do I know if I've got it? If I do, how do I use it? Not to worry. If you allow it, it will happen.

For example, I attended a meeting in which the senior management team of a privately held boutique pharmaceuticals company was introducing the firm to an assembly of bankers and other potential investors in advance of an eventual IPO. The chairman and founder was unable to attend. He was laid up 3,000 miles away in a California hospital recovering from surgery to fix a broken leg suffered in a rock-climbing accident several days earlier.

Speaking for him and for the company was a young team of presentable professional managers, the CEO, CFO, and head of marketing and sales, who proceeded to underwhelm. The meeting, scheduled for an hour, wound up taking more than two. If they had a story to tell, they didn't seem to know what it was. They got lost in minutiae jammed onto complex slides and never dragged their eyes up from presentation books, reading straight off the page while endless word slides kept marching across the screen behind them. Worse, they spoke in the secret handshake language of the discipline, leaving most of the bankers clueless. Not surprising, a fair number of investors slipped out before the droning finally stopped.

To put it kindly, there was no spark of creativity to be found anywhere in the presentation. Far from it. What we saw and heard was predictable, boring, and nearly incomprehensible. If there was an ounce of leadership anywhere in that team, we couldn't find it.

When the laid-up chairman found out what happened, he hit the roof and vowed to come to New York himself to set things right. Energized, the bankers rushed to arrange another meeting and managed to persuade most of the wary investors to return for what could only be described as a kind of rerun.

But what greeted the investors the second time around a month later was nothing like the sleepy fox trot they had endured on the first go-through. This time the chairman, now fully recovered, led the show while his management team simply listened (and later helped to answer questions). The difference was stunning.

For starters, he knew his story, and he knew how to tell it. The story was simple, but like most simple stories it was powerful. The story was that the company had developed an anticancer drug for certain women's cancers that was three times as effective as the leading cancer drug on the market but only one-third as toxic. The drug was in Phase II clinical trials and expected to pass Phase III in three months. In effect, he was saying that the company was about to serve up a blockbuster that would turn the billion-dollar chemotherapy industry upside down. This seemed to come as news to the entire audience, which from that point on gave the chairman their undivided attention. It was all over in 25 minutes. Nobody was surprised when the IPO sold way above expectations on the first round.

The only person surprised was the chairman, who afterwards privately expressed dismay that his own people didn't seem to understand the story—a failure that by itself would have cost the company the biggest opportunity of its relatively short life. It was a lesson not lost on the chairman. By the time the show did hit the road, the show itself was a kind of blockbuster, and the management team was unrecognizable. They were as articulate, engaging, and focused as the chairman. Gone were the tiresome functionaries, replaced now by three confident corporate officers who almost overnight had begun to look and sound like leaders. Second only to the compelling investment proposition (the story) and the attractive financials, the big selling point with investors was the solidly impressive management team.

How do you measure the business value of this perception? You can't. But in this case I would venture that the value might have been worth half the initial offering, or a little over $60 million.

In fact, in business, perception is priceless. At analyst meetings, where the stakes are high and perception can save the day, you are more likely to hear one analyst say to another, "What did you think of the CEO?" rather than, "What did you think of what the CEO had to say?"

As everyone knows, Donald Trump is a CEO with a lot to say and one of the most creative business artists ever. Some people might argue that he is more of a "illusionist," but no one would deny he is creative. Year after year he magically overcomes challenges that would overwhelm other less inspired CEOs. Year after year he rolls out ingenious rescue missions to pull vulnerable assets and shaky deals back from the brink of total collapse.

It's an act marvelous to behold, and it's more than just mirrors.

Trump's trump card is an unparalleled talent for negotiation, coupled with robust self-confidence and impressive selling skills.

On any given day, Trump—who, you may recall, wrote a book entitled, *The Art of the Deal*—is juggling pieces of his gaming and real estate empire, working the phones to appease creditors, lecturing bankers, and soothing anxious investors.

And as stakes intensify and pressures mount, he only seems to get better.

For example, with his entire gaming business sliding toward bankruptcy and his crown jewel casino, The Trump Taj Mahal, at serious risk, Trump simply does what he always does: He shmoozes. He huddles with his bankers yet again, renegotiates yet again, and the problem seems to go away yet again until next month or next year.

And is Donald Trump worried?

"Me, worry?" he says. "Are you kidding?"

Everyone knows that as long as "The Donald" can still talk, his empire is secure.

But security is a luxury few artists can afford or even sustain. In the world of freewheeling enterprise, security is a prize often won at the lectern or standing on a stage or in a meeting room.

At a recent conference of venture capitalists and other investors, I witnessed a stunning example of how a little imagination and artistry can go a long way.

Two young CEOs were trying to woo venture capitalists on what each believed to be proprietary technology but what was in fact very similar technology designed to enhance WiFi computing range and picture quality for cell phones and other handheld devices.

What happened is a telling lesson in human nature.

When it came time for the first CEO to make his presentation, he positioned himself behind a lectern, put on his reading glasses, stuck his head down into his text, and never looked up again for the next 40 minutes—20 minutes longer than his allotted time. His pitch—what we could hear or understand of it—boiled down to an exhaustive dissertation on the technology behind the product. By the time he finally finished, we were just thankful it was over and couldn't wait to take a break.

During the break—and this is important—there was virtually no buzz. The VCs worked their cell phones and Blackberries, but no one talked about what they all had just seen and heard.

After the break, we stepped into a different world. Someone at the door was handing out camera-equipped cell phones. The lights were low. The screen behind the stage was filled with images of swimming fish, as if we were visitors inside a giant aquarium. The picture was startlingly lifelike. A reggae beat came from somewhere. Bob Marley? The music got more intense.

Suddenly a man—the company CEO—appeared on stage wearing a yellow tee shirt with a stylized fish across the front. On the back we could see the word *WAHOO* in large letters.

"Ladies and gentlemen, welcome to the future," the CEO said. At that, the lights went up, and we saw ourselves as he swept the camera slowly back and forth over the crowd.

Then every cell phone in the room rang at once. When we answered the call, the picture on the wall changed—first to the *WAHOO* fish logo and then to us—the audience. On stage, the CEO pulled back a curtain to reveal an eighty-gallon fish tank. We saw that the same camera cell phone he now held in his hand was the same one that had been photographing the fish and was now aimed at us—not in single images but in streaming video on the wall and on our hand-held screens.

But the fun had only just begun. He went on to show, via live demonstrations and DVD images, the full range of capabilities and applications of the Wahoo prototype. Anyone who had listened carefully to the presentation just before the break would realize that the very capabilities we were witnessing here echoed the previous pitch, with minor variations.

And yet the results could not have been more different. Yes, the second presentation was manipulative. Yes, it was high risk: The technology might have failed at a crucial moment, or the VCs might have viewed the whole thing as unnecessary and superficial. And yes, some of the VCs might have viewed with disapproval the showy stagecraft and obvious expense of just putting the pitch together in the first place.

But that's not what happened. The VCs, it turned out, enjoyed the fun-loving approach, the edgy attitude. And with few exceptions they actually appreciated the entertainment value behind the information. The buzz was on even before we left the room.

Creativity, it turned out, was the decisive factor, and Wahoo won the VC dollars hands down.

What I'm trying to say here is that if we allow it, the creative mind has measurable business value and will reveal itself. Creativity is an asset often overlooked and little understood but highly prized. Creative thinkers make great businesspeople. And investors and customers alike *perceive* creativity, or evidence of it, as an attractive proposition. CVA coupled with creativity spells profitability.

> Creativity is an asset often overlooked and little understood but highly prized.

13

WHO'S DRIVING?

I f you want to lead successfully, it's important to know who you are, what you actually do, and what you stand for. This sounds obvious, but the truth is that many people are so deep in their professional lives, they're shocked to discover that the person they think they are is a stranger they created. These people have two lives—one at work and the other away from work. For the most part, the stranger lives at work. Sometimes the line between work and nonwork vanishes altogether so that work itself consumes every waking hour. That's when the stranger takes over. That's when you have trouble remembering the other person you thought you were. This can be problematic because the stranger may be successful but not necessarily the person in the deepest sense you feel you really are or want to be.

If you happen to lead, this schizophrenic approach to life and work can get in the way of forward movement. Too much energy is expended keeping up appearances, and in the end, no artifice, no matter how clever, can substitute for the real thing. The only answer is to reverse the situation. The answer is to make certain that the person at work is not your creation. The person at work and in life itself should always be the person you feel you really are.

This person is comfortable with himself and comfortable with his employees, customers, and investors. He's the same person in the office as he is in the kitchen at home or in a bar having a beer with a friend. This person is the authentic you, so he was never created by you. There's no second face or second voice masking the true you, no artificial, if cleverly disguised, barrier at the point of transaction or connection.

There comes a point in everyone's life when there is no longer a need to present the stranger to the world. In the case of any leader, this point should come sooner rather than later. To use a Dr. Jekyll and Mr. Hyde analogy, it is better to be the competent, driven, smart Dr. Jekyll than an equally competent, driven, and smart Mr. Hyde.

With Mr. Hyde out of the way, new possibilities rush in. They arrive on the wings of a very profitable, if little acknowledged, phenomenon I call *business likability*.

Business likability is a reality business leaders can't afford to do without. As media guru Marshall McLuhan observed years ago, you are the message. Everybody wants to do business with people they not only like but also respect and admire (you've got a good jump on the second two if you've already got the first).

> **Business likability is a reality business leaders can't afford to do without.**

Business likability comes in two flavors. The first variety is likely to eventually self-destruct. Here are some examples:

- Senior Vice President Marcia is a hit with her customers but bombs with her family. She's alienated her kids and is contemplating divorce.

- Team leader John has a lot of friends at work, but outside work he's a loner.
- Account manager Harold is a social butterfly, but at work he's introspective, secretive, makes no effort to form friends or alliances, and sticks pretty much to himself—with one exception: Put him in front of an audience, and he becomes another person: crisp, interesting, articulate, on top of his subject.

> **Every leader knows that the closer to the top we get, the more our social and professional lives seem to blend.**

What these people lack is consistency. In a sense, they are two people. To some degree they lead two different lives. But every leader knows that the closer to the top we get, the more our social and professional lives seem to blend. Alliances are created, and deals are done on the golf course, at the cocktail party and beach, and in the conference room. Who we are on the golf course is the same person people expect us to be at the office. The next transaction, even our career, may depend on it.

This is why we need to know who we are.

One CEO I know won't hire a senior employee until he first plays a round of golf with that person. I am no golfer myself, but this CEO claims that he can tell everything he needs to know about a person's character and problem-solving, management, and social skills simply by being with him for a few hours on the links (you know if a Mr. Hyde is hiding in there someplace, he's likely to pop up at some point during a golf game).

We need to know not only what we *do*, but *why* we do it because it should go without saying that in order to feel fulfilled in any leadership capacity, we've got to have a sense of purpose. A job without purpose is only a job, and a large number of people will tell you they're only collecting a paycheck. But we'd like to think the person writing the paycheck will tell you that his motivation goes beyond just getting paid. Sometimes these people are hard to find, but it's interesting how many of them wind up at or near the top. Even self-serving motivation, if it advances the interests of the company, has merit.

Take the case of an acquaintance of mine, an engineer at a large defense contractor, who rises through the ranks to become the vice president of an operating company making supersecret electronic detection gear. Ask anybody in the company, and they'll tell you he's a great guy. When he talks at employee gatherings and other company events, he never uses notes, and he always leaves his audiences feeling good about themselves and the company—even when things aren't going well and he's talking tough love and trouble (when he inherited the job, trouble meant quality-control problems). He's good with names, often taking the time to stop and chat, even in the middle of a busy day. To listen to him speak, you'd almost believe that he is having *fun*. His message is: *Do* sweat the small stuff. Quality is the name of the game in this business, and our jobs—and the lives of the people who use our products—depend on little details like precise calibration and solid fit.

He repeats this message every chance he gets, frequently delivering it personally and face to face. Surveys reveal that quality is up across the board, and now, orders are on the rise. He's got reasons to believe things will continue to get better, reasons that he shares in e-mails and closed-circuit TV appearances he tapes regularly and broadcasts to employees in every facility. In fact, workers at all levels have come to rely on him for personal updates that constantly monitor the company's health.

More than once he's joked that he's only collecting a paycheck like everybody else. You suspect he may be only half-joking—but nobody cares. You get the impression he loves what he's doing and, more important, that he's looking out for everybody in the organization from the bottom up.

In other words, he's got business likability. This same likability is perceived by customers, subcontractors, and government and military officials.

Once we understand who we really are and the true motivation behind our work, then we ought to stand for something.

If we're going to stand for something, we've got to have a voice. Years ago, onetime Xerox CEO David Kearns stood for better education. His clarion call was, "Wake up, America—We need to do a better job educating our children." Kearns was alarmed by the steady rise of illiteracy among young people and the slide in math scores. Time and again he warned that America's future competitiveness was in peril. He spoke often and always on the same topic. Education became a national issue thanks in large part to his constant public lobbying for remedies and remains a volatile subject to this day.

Kearns' leadership legacy is not defined by his tenure at the helm of Xerox but as a champion of education. It was perhaps not coincidental that the education theme happened to fold nicely into Xerox's history of research and development and the company's positioning as a leader in what some people were starting to call the "knowledge industry."

A Republican presidential candidate once boiled his entire campaign down to just two words: flat tax. Even today when people think flat tax, they think Steve Forbes. Ted Turner's famous act of largesse was the biggest-ever private gift to the United Nations, which realized only a portion of the $1 billion windfall before Ted got nicked when the telecom bubble burst. (The U.N. may have to wait a long time for the rest.) In the meantime, Ted has become a kind of commercial for the U.N.

Bill Gates wants to see a Windows-loaded computing device in the hands of every kid in every school in the world, so one of his favorite public projects is the digitization of the classroom (which happens to fit nicely with his corporate objectives).

One client of mine confessed he felt a little daunted when he was tapped to head a regional financial services company whose former CEO was both dynamic and celebrated. My client knew that he could not top his predecessor's act, at least not on the charisma scale, but he understood the wisdom of acquiring a public presence and did want to be seen and heard. So he set out trying to determine if there was a cause or banner he felt strongly enough about to call his own. He made a short list, talked to his family and friends, and finally hit on an issue that he and his wife both embraced. He decided he would be a champion for clean air and water.

Air pollution and water pollution were not official items on his company's agenda or part of his three-year plan, but they were an excuse to stand up and be heard on any number of occasions where he might be asked to speak, and they were issues he had always felt passionate about. Once he committed himself, he became unstoppable. His staff found opportunities for him to tell his story, and he began to establish himself as a regional voice on something close to his heart. The company sponsored kayak races and sky diving events, among other things, and soon the concepts of clean air and clean water became inseparable from the company itself. Even the advertising started to feature beautiful photographs of lakes, rivers, and endless blue skies.

Business exploded, and in two years the company's performance eclipsed the best years of his predecessor. He became something of a local celebrity, and the fact that he was a businessperson who spoke out on pollution didn't hurt his business likability with the man on the street.

It was all good for business, and it was all about finding a signature voice.

This is why it's important to know who you are, what you actually do, and what you stand for.

CHAPTER

THE WINNER'S CIRCLE

B ecause you're a team player doesn't mean you shouldn't be part of the dream team, or even a star. By definition, being a star means doing things differently. In the context of CVA, being different usually means performing better—wherever you may be seen and heard—in meetings, presentations, reviews, and negotiations. Different is good. Who will fault you for being crisp, interesting, inspiring, and memorable? Who will complain if you get your message across in half the time but twice as effectively as the next guy? In fact, if you're a leader, or want to be, you might disappoint if you don't do these things and more.

Take the case of the Fortune 20 industrial giant that every year holds a conference of its top 600 business leaders and managers at the same big hotel in Florida. It's a kind of annual rite of passage, and every year, 30 or so managers are tapped to speak. This assignment can be both exhilarating and intimidating. It can be the rocket that accelerates your career or the torpedo that sinks it.

So it's not surprising that when people get the word that it's time for them to step up to the plate, serious preparation ensues. It's not unusual, for example, for some people to begin putting their thoughts together almost a year in advance. Yet, ironically, for all their trouble, most of the players wind up looking and sounding pretty much the same. Several days later it might be nearly impossible to recall who said what because most of the presentations are nearly identical. To pick a number, if you're talking about 30 presentations, yours could get lost in the shuffle—unless you're the one who fires up the CVA.

Getting lost in the crowd is not a good idea for self-starters looking to break out of the pack (after all, the other 29 potentially may be competitors for the same job). This is an observation not lost on a fraction of the annual presenters who manage to shine because they don't look and sound like everybody else. Interestingly, not everyone in the audience can tell you exactly *why* these people are different. All the people in the audience know for sure is that they are impressed. Better yet, they remember not only the names and faces of the few memorable presenters but also what the presentations were about. By contrast, most of them will tell you that the rest of the program (what with golf and cocktails) is pretty much a blur.

In the end, the conference accomplishes what it sets out to do in the first place—to serve as an off-site forum for global managers to meet and talk face to face in one place for a few days once a year.

But a small handful of players has accomplished much more. For these select few, their careers will never be the same because the senior management team is now talking about what a great job they did at the conference Within months, the buzz will result in new assignments for two and talk of promotion for another three.

If you were to go back and analyze what made the few so much more effective, you'd see important distinctions.

For example, the guy an hour ago, a general manager and high potential, pretty much put everybody to sleep. He was up there talking about best practices—how he and his people had centralized an international distribution network. When he finally got to it, it was a legitimate message, but he still managed to tune out the vast majority of his listeners.

Here's how it went: First, he said, "Good morning" and insisted everybody say "Good morning" back. Then he took some time to say how much he appreciated the opportunity to be there, and then he thanked the organizers, and then he showed his agenda for his "presentation" and read it off the wall line for line. Now he's had the stage for three or four minutes, and we still don't know anything. People are checking their Blackberries and starting to take out their *Wall Street Journals*.

It gets worse. He's reading right out of a prepared text at the podium, talking about the history of the parent company as a precursor leading to a discussion surrounding intimate details of the technology, such as an elaborate review of a GPS freight-tagging process that is part of the success of the new distribution system. But before he can even get that far, the audience is starting to chafe because eight minutes into this thing he still hasn't told them about the new distribution system itself, or why it matters, or what his bottom line really is. The bottom line, of course, is that this particular best practice is increasing speed, efficiency, profitability, and customer satisfaction. These improvements, in turn, are contributing to cost savings and revenue growth.

And that's all that anybody in that audience cares about. They want to know just three things: Are we making money? Are we saving money? And if you have something that can help me or my business, just let me know.

But that message—the only message that matters—is too long in coming. The result is that the presentation is rear-weighted. In other words, if there's anything worth knowing, we're not going to hear it or see it until somewhere near the end, if at all. He's also loading the huge screens behind him with one tedious word slide after another, interspersed with a ton of charts, tables, and schematics. By the time he's finally done talking, people are fidgeting and thinking about a break. They're also thinking it took an hour to make a business point that virtually anybody in the audience can sum up in less than 15 seconds.

This guy is followed immediately by another high potential whose style is noticeably different. For starters, she forgoes the podium and chooses instead to walk the stage. She's talking about acquiring a Korean company that makes a ballistics-grade plastic laminate that can be used in car windows, police vests, sports products, and a host of other applications. This technology folds in nicely with the products and services of the parent company. The Korean company has several other breakthrough products in the pipeline, and projections for rapid growth are good.

When she starts talking, she skips the usual amenities and gets right to the point: The acquired technology will make the parent company an overnight player in a vital portion of its portfolio that had not seen significant growth in more than six years.

Behind her, there's nothing to distract: no word slides, no charts, just a logo. Now the logo disappears, and she's showing a slow-motion DVD of a fist-sized ball of steel plowing into a ¼-inch thick pane of the laminate at 1200 feet per second. Then there's another shot of a Korean shooting at another Korean just 10 feet away. The bullet splats against the laminate, and both Koreans smile.

But this presentation is not all fun and games. Now it's time to talk financials and projections. For the next eight minutes, more conventional-looking charts and tables start popping up on the screens. But here we notice three differences: First, the slides are simpler, the images larger (just one chart per slide), and the colors more attractive. Second, every slide only reinforces the theme of growth. Third, this person actually makes her point before she shows the slide that supports that point. We also notice that there aren't so many slides, so the presentation is shorter and looks a lot less cluttered. We notice one more thing. When the slide portion is finished, the logo pops back up, and she wraps it up with a strong ending that reinforces the theme.

Without sacrificing substance, the presentation is a hit. The effect on her audience couldn't be more different than the sense of ho-hum that had numbed the room just a half-hour earlier. She'll be asked to give it again in a series of corporate departmental meetings—but not each will look like the other. In one, she'll start with the DVD of the ball of steel hitting the plastic laminate. In another, she'll start with a story about how a couple of Israelis recently showed up in her office with a blank check to license the same technology in Israel for use in Israeli Air Force F-16s. In another, she'll simply tell them the entire message right at the top and forge on from there.

And best of all, she can do the whole thing in just 20 minutes.

It's important to keep in mind that both the individuals we're comparing here are intelligent and competent managers. Both are viewed as potential future leaders of the company. But one leaves a footprint in the minds of her listeners, whereas the other does not. One can be an inspiration, whereas the other can be an exasperation. Given that both have solid reputations and good track records, which do you think will be more likely to rise?

If nothing else, people will come to appreciate the one they view to be the more inspiring simply because she's the one who knows the story, makes it memorable, and doesn't take more time than she has to to tell it. She's the one her peers and superiors will come to think of as the articulate executive, and she's the one who will keep coming to mind every time there's another promotion opportunity on the way.

FIRE CONTROL

If an executive manages to rally support but finds himself clashing with another company leader within his own firm, all bets are off until hostilities are resolved. In fact, butting heads at the top can mean shaking things up at the bottom line—or worse.

For example, two senior executives of a major international company have a long-standing disagreement. Employees and customers know they don't get along, which is bad for business. The younger guy has taken over as CEO, but still has to report to the older guy, who has been running the company and now serves as chairman of the board.

The chairman often "interferes" with the new executive's work. Among other things, he tells him what to do and pressures him to make the numbers. So the CEO naturally resents that he's not entirely trusted. On top of that, he has some policy differences with the chairman, which they have been unable to resolve because they don't communicate very often or very well.

The result is that they're log-jammed on an accounting issue that will soon come back to bite them. The question is how to value some of the company's assets and whether the current method is even accurate. This is obviously an important policy matter that deserves careful, detailed analysis. But because the CEO and chairman are so polarized in their views and tend to argue when the subject comes up, they have not commissioned the kind of objective fiduciary staff analysis they should have.

The upshot is that the problem festers so long, outsiders—including analysts—come to believe the company is hiding something or, worse, hiding to mislead investors.

Finally, the inevitable happens: A news story breaks highlighting the issue, and both guys are suddenly cast into the glare of public scrutiny. Their only defense is that their conflict, which is now public knowledge, has prevented them from taking appropriate action and moving ahead.

It's a lame answer but all they've got, and as a result, follow-up stories appear in the press, and the stock slides, losing 25 percent of its value in just three days.

These are the kinds of boneheaded egocentrics at the expense of shareholders that must be avoided at all costs, according to Alex Hiam, author of *Taming the Conflict Dragon*.

The solution: In this case, the conflict was allowed to fester too long, and both executives wound up being forced to resign. But if they hadn't been pushed out, they would have needed to get together and issue a joint apology in which they explained that disagreements and lousy communications were responsible for the problem and that they were working together to resolve it.

The better solution, according to Hiam, would have been to avoid the catastrophe in the first place simply by resolving to forbid egos on either side from ever coming between the company and its employees and shareholders. An agreement to conduct a thorough analysis of the accounting issue and a willingness to meet and talk would have helped, too. In the end, doing the obvious and talking would have saved both jobs, preserved the wealth of the company, and kept shareholders from jumping ship.

Sometimes the clash occurs not at the top but somewhere in the middle, as in this situation:

Bob, the head of sales for the largest and most profitable division of a giant industrial company, is a passionate believer in relationship selling. He loves to press the flesh and get in front of customers at every opportunity. As he likes to point out in staff meetings with the division president, sales—unlike marketing—always produces bottom-line profit.

This does not sit well with Jane, the head of marketing, who also reports directly to the president. She's a professional with big ad agency experience who recently joined the company to boost brand image and to help grow market share. She thinks that Bob and his people are uncooperative and old-fashioned, and she's lobbied successfully for the division to shift more of its spending out of direct sales and into advertising.

Bob and Jane have concluded independently that each could do without the other. Neither has made any overtures of good will, and on the occasions when they do have to meet, they are mutually cordial but icy. Bob views Jane as a threat. Jane views Bob as an obstacle. Bob thinks Jane is a shrewish operator out to steal turf at his expense. Jane thinks Bob is a back-slapping empty suit. Tension and mistrust build to the point where any thought of constructive communication is so unappealing that it's out of the question.

Unfortunately, the major golf tournament the company sponsors every year is coming up soon. Both Bob and Jane are jockeying for the pole position. It's a great chance not only to entertain clients but also to boost brand image and fatten market share. So they're forced to meet in one tense sitdown to work out funding for the event. But they can only argue. Feelings are high, and everyone within earshot and eyeshot can see it's become personal.

As the deadline looms, the president convenes a staff meeting and asks how plans for the event are coming. Bob gives his version, and Jane presents hers. Right away the president sees that there's virtually no coordination, teamwork, or unity. Even the budgets conflict. Jane emphasizes money for media, whereas Bob wants the lion's share of available funds to go to events and customer entertainment.

The president sours. Later he calls them both into his office and reads them the riot act. He tells them that if they can't cooperate he'll replace them both.

In the end, the golf tournament comes off without a hitch. But the careers of both executives have been needlessly placed in jeopardy, and both reputations have been damaged enough so that it will require a real show of cooperation in the future and a lot of fence mending before all is forgiven and forgotten.

As Hiam says, the resolution of this conflict is so simple, even a child could have figured it out. Lessons learned:

1. Sharing information for the purpose of meeting a goal is better than wasting time arguing.
2. Instead of turning backs on each other, each could have shown leadership by looking for more, not less communication.
3. Instead of hammering on differences, they should have looked for ways to combine strengths.
4. Failing to work out differences before staff meetings is a real mistake.
5. Collaboration between team members is always more productive than confrontation.
6. When two functions have potential synergies to begin with, one and one makes three.

Even when outright hostility is not the issue, autonomous rule can still cause train wrecks. When two divisions of a large media conglomerate went after the same acquisition target, the result was embarrassment and failure. The prize went to a third suitor. After that, heads rolled, and management installed communication and coordination protocols that should have been there in the first place.

One of the world's most admired companies had customers up in arms because the left hand didn't seem to know what the right was doing. One industrial division was doing business with several customers, apparently unaware that the same customers were also doing business with a separate division. Shipments were mishandled or delayed, invoices lost, and service interrupted. Ill will and anger ran rampant. One customer defected in disgust when problems weren't fixed fast enough. All totaled, the company lost tens of millions of dollars. This breakdown in processes could have been avoided if the divisions simply had thought to share customer information.

Confronted with a choice between costly mayhem and a profitable combination of strengths, which would you pick?

Internal damage control begins at the top. When things are going well and the company is making money, it's easy to overlook discord. But the penalty for neglect can eclipse temporary benefits, as we've seen time and again when companies implode. A top-tier Wall Street firm came unglued after a period of unprecedented prosperity simply because the chairman was too busy making acquisitions to supervise department heads, who viewed one another as competitors rather than collaborators. They didn't talk much, shared little, and fought for the same customers.

Eventually, this lapse in leadership drove down productivity to the point where the bank became uncompetitive. The result was the ouster of the chairman and installation of a new leader who dismantled the whole unwieldy apparatus and started again, almost from scratch.

If you're an executive, you understand that conflict in business is routine. In fact, business often *is* conflict. Beyond departmental rivalries, you've got supplier and customer negotiations, frequent disagreements about what to do or how to do it, and even interpersonal issues such as having to work with someone you don't like or who doesn't like you. These issues are so ubiquitous that you can take some small comfort in the knowledge that your competition is having to deal with them too.

But left ignored or unmanaged, they can throw both you and your organization *out* of the competition.

To make sure you're managing conflict to your advantage and not letting conflict orchestrate your ruin, Hiam has these commonsense suggestions:

1. *First, deal with the conflict.* Don't try to finish the project, make the decision, or write the plan until you first come to a resolution. Most of us like to think that we'll take care of the problem later, when we have more time. There's never more time.

2. *Talk openly about the difficult stuff.* Don't be shy about digging right down into the nasty broth burbling right under the surface. For example, a manager seems irritated and says little in a meeting. You ask her to talk with you afterwards, and it turns out that she's upset because she thinks another manager has exaggerated progress on a project and padded sales data to avoid trouble with the boss. Now that you know what's going on, you resolve the problem before it has a chance to escalate into a real mess.

3. *Listen.* Hiam is talking here about what psychologists call *emphatic* listening, which is based on the proposition that you will never get to the root cause of any conflict by talking at people. Ask interested, nonthreatening questions (i.e., "Is there another approach we should be looking at?") Then sit back, keep it zipped, resist the temptation to butt in, don't try to fill awkward pauses—and see what happens.

4. *Focus on underlying needs—not stated demands.* For example, a supplier says, "We have to have a price increase." But that's not necessarily true. What's true is that the supplier's costs

have gone up. The underlying need is that it costs too much to make the product. So you send a team of your people to sit down with a team of design engineers from the supplier and—surprise—together they come up with a redesigned product that's lighter but stronger and uses fewer parts. This allows the supplier to achieve economies of scale. No more need for a price increase. Win-win.

5. *Be creative.* Some very smart people choose to see conflicts not as problems but as opportunities. That's because any time two people or groups clash, both sides own the problem. When you double the talent and the brainpower in a given situation, some surprisingly creative and interesting results can occur. And that's when a problem can become a solution.

So tame that dragon. Don't let conflict become the boss of you because it will—if you ignore it, or don't know how to wrestle it to the ground, or fail to see the opportunities that might grow from it.

RULES OF THE ROAD

16

TAKING THE POLE POSITION

A s I've been saying, to morph from competent manager to articulate executive and group leader requires more than an understanding of business. You've also got to harness the power of business
communications.

If you're not by nature a born leader, it's important that you learn
leadership behaviors—beginning with the art of plain talk.

The fundamentals are easy. Earlier I talked about how the perfect
presentation—or book, play, or novel—is made up of just five compo-
nents: strong start, one theme, good examples, ordinary language, and
strong ending. That's the *POWER formula* (see Chapter 4).

In a business environment—a world of meetings and presentations—there's another requisite, which we might call the *foundation*.
The POWER formula rests on the foundation, which has only three parts:

1. Always begin and end any presentation without slides.

2. Get rid of most word slides (but keep them in the digital document or hard copy). If you choose to use slides, make sure that they are all charts, tables, graphics, schematics, sketches, or photos and that they connect to the theme.
3. Introduce the next slide while the previous slide is still up.

As simple and effective as these rules are, people all across the United States and around the world violate them every day mostly because they don't know they exist. This oversight can be a drag on earnings potential and personal success.

Take the example of the team of hard-charging bankers (four junior people and two managing directors) who fly to Chicago from New York to pitch a big insurance company on a transaction worth about $15 million in fees.

It isn't until the last moment, when they are actually on the elevator, that they start trying to figure out who's going to take the lead. Who's going to handle which section of the presentation? What's the message? How should we end it?

They are greeted in the lobby by executives from the company's senior management team. Everybody introduces themselves, and the bankers are ushered into a wood-paneled conference room with a nice view of Chicago and Lake Michigan. After they all take their seats, one of the managing directors takes the lead. He says good morning (again), reintroduces himself, and then tells the insurance execs how happy the bankers are to be in Chicago and how much they appreciate having this opportunity to make this presentation. He spends the next two minutes reintroducing the bankers and then asks everyone to open their presentation books to page one, a word slide, which he proceeds to read, word for word. He fails to notice that his would-be clients on the other side of the table are already flipping pages and seem to be looking for information toward the back of the book, which is almost the size of the Chicago White Pages.

The managing director is now reading the second page, another word slide, when one of the insurance execs interrupts and asks a question. The managing director seems taken aback, uncertain how to respond, glances for help down the table, and seeing none, quickly suggests they will get to that issue, and then he continues to read from the book—and never gets to the issue.

The insurance people are getting the message. But it's not the message the bankers have in mind. The insurance guys are thinking the bankers are (1) not familiar with their material, (2) not fully informed about the background or history of the insurance company, (3) unaware of the needs of the insurance company, (4) not behaving like a team, and (5) grievously ill-prepared.

In any case, the insurance people are now targeting specific numbers buried in the back of the book that they were interested in, and a private conversation is underway between the CFO and CIO on the other side of the table.

It is now becoming clear beyond any reasonable doubt that the bankers are just slinging another boiler plate, that they have no relevant message, and that they are obviously interested only in their own case, since they don't seem to have a clue about what the other side really wants or needs.

When the banker finally finishes his trek through the word slides, he says, "If you would please turn to page 12 of your books, I'd now like to turn the presentation over to Bob who will. . . ." Bob takes the hand-off but seems a little uneasy, as if he's not familiar with the material. And there's little connection with what Bob is supposed to be talking about and what the clients just heard from the managing director. Bob's presentation is so inept that the managing director cuts in abruptly and finishes the section himself—23 pages later.

The insurance people are losing their patience. But they still try to be gracious. So they resist the temptation to ask the bankers to get to the point. Now the managing director turns to another junior person and says something like, "And now I'd like to ask Tom to talk about the capital structure and fiduciary obligations." But Tom falters, saying, "I think Bill may know more about that." He adds quickly, "But I could talk about debt issues."

The managing director can scarcely control his anger. He turns to Bill, who sheepishly says that he, too, is unprepared to talk about capital structure and fiduciary obligations. Bill seems flustered. He mutters, "I think I got a little lost. What page are we on?"

The managing director glares at him.

The junior guy, trying not to show his mounting panic, breaks the silence with, "I'll do it. I just need to know what page we're on."

Rather than appear rude, the insurers let the presentation drag on. They ask a number of pointed questions along the way, which the bankers are not capable of answering to their satisfaction.

Eventually, the presentation just peters out, with the bankers getting a noxious sense that things are not going well. The boat is sinking. They know they're drowning. The insurance guys are poker-faced, but their eyes reveal disappointment. At the end, the lead banker asserts without any real conviction that his bank is the best partner for this transaction. But both sides know otherwise. By now both sides understand that given how things have gone in this meeting, that isn't really the case and never will be.

Needless to say, the bankers do not win the account. In fact, the experience leaves such a bad taste that they are unable to get in the door again.

While this story may seem a little extreme, it actually happened— and as anyone who has been in business knows, similar situations are not uncommon.

If you multiply this scene a million times, you may get some idea of the staggering amount of money and opportunity we are all leaving on the table every day. Even a child can tell you that just the most rudimentary preparation and forethought, coupled with at least a token amount of practice, could have reversed the outcome. In other words, can an hour potentially be worth $15 million?

The answer is very possibly.

To make that answer a definite yes, we have to throw in a knowledge of the architecture and foundation I mentioned a minute ago.

Suppose, for example, the meeting had gone something like this: Two managing directors and one less senior person (perhaps the "coverage" person) arrive on the executive floor. They're greeted by the insurance execs. At this point both sides get the introductions out of the way and move on to the conference room. If the insurance people want to socialize, chitchat, or continue to talk about the weather, that's fine. But this warm-up should occur, if possible, while everybody is still standing, in "prepresentation mode," if you will. Now let's say that everybody sits down, and the insurance guys seem to want to have a little more socializing. That's fine, too. The bankers should be alert to the insurance people's leads in whatever direction they want to go and whatever mood they happen to be in. These bankers are happy to partake of the relaxed approach as long as that is what the clients signal they want. But the moment the chitchat has run its course, the lead banker seizes the first opportunity to get right down to business.

Getting right down to business means beginning with something perhaps unexpected and getting the other side sitting a little straighter in their chairs.

The insurance people have asked to have the presentation book in their hands at the meeting, so they've got copies in front of them. But these copies are so skinny they look like they're on a starvation diet. They are less than a third of an inch thick, with only five charts and no word slides. Before the insurance people can open the book, the lead banker says, "Before we open the book, there's something I'd like to say first."

Now he's got everybody's attention. But instead of piddling away his moment of greatest impact with something predictably inane like, "Good morning, it's a pleasure to be here today. We appreciate having this opportunity," he says something like, "Our message is very simple." Then he proceeds to give them that simple message, which anticipates and answers the client's needs (growth, capital restructuring, debt refinancing, acquisitions) in less than 30 seconds.

As they listen, the insurance people notice right away that the banker—unlike some of the other sales teams that have been by recently—makes no mention of his bank. Everything he says seems to be focused on just one thing: the insurance company. Instead of talking about how great the bank is, he's telling them what he thinks the bank can do for the insurance company. Instead of talking about the history of the bank, he's talking about the future of the insurance company. Instead of walking them through an agenda, he's already hit the bottom line: Help the insurance company be more productive, grow, run a smarter business, cut costs, and make more money.

This banker has everybody's undivided attention—and we haven't even opened the book yet. In other words, this banker is adhering to the one precept that must prevail in every sales presentation: Serve the client. It's amazing how many people forget this basic tenet but not so amazing that many fail because they don't.

The banker spends the last couple of minutes putting into motion another little secret known to only the most successful sales, professional, and businesspeople for whom an important part of the job is presentation.

The secret is this: They give their entire presentation before they show even the first chart, just in case they run out of time or are interrupted—and because they know that capturing the audience psychologically in the first few minutes is going to be the decisive factor determining whether they succeed.

So far the banker has achieved the first two of the five principles of the POWER formula. He has started strongly, and he's established his theme.

In this case, his theme is straightforward: Here's the problem you have, and here's exactly what we think we can do to fix it. When he speaks, he says *you* more than he says *I* or *we*. The insurance people don't know it, but in just 2 minutes and 40 seconds they've heard everything they need to know to make a decision in favor of hiring the bank. This is simply an abbreviated version of what otherwise might have taken 40 minutes. But there's more. The banker knows that if these decision makers had to walk out of the room right now, he could take comfort that he had said in just a few minutes what he wanted them to hear, and nothing less.

Like a good lawyer, he has made a compelling case—again, having a real understanding of the problems and an equally clear view of the solution. So far he has laid the case out for all to see. He's offered several brief real-life anecdotes to make it clear that his bank has been down this road before and tackled successfully the same challenges with other clients in similar situations.

Now, like a good lawyer, he's about to prove his case by providing evidence. This proof comes in the form of data, actual examples, charts, and tables (no word slides). These charts and tables are kept to a bare minimum and are justifiable as evidence only if they support the theme and serve to further press the message. The pictures are line charts, pie charts, and step charts. They are all color-consistent, simply designed, and easy to read. Each diagram is chosen carefully to make just one business point, and the charts, taken together, drive the theme.

The insurance guys are impressed. It's clear that these bankers (at least so far) know something about their insurance company, do their due diligence, know what's important, and understand how to make themselves useful. The decision makers are more than willing to continue to pay attention.

Now they see something that they've never seen before. Suddenly the lead banker simply stops talking, and without any introduction and without missing a beat, the junior banker, David, picks up where the lead banker leaves off. It's a seamless transition with no apparent signal at all, and it only serves to reinforce the notion that these bankers really do operate as a team—so much so, in fact, that they're able to pass the baton in an unbroken dialogue. The managing director doesn't even bother to look at the junior banker during the handoff. The clients are sitting up even straighter.

The clients are noticing something else: Even though the other side is doing all the talking, they feel like they're participating in a *conversation*, not listening to a *lecture* or *presentation*. This is not only unexpected but also enormously appealing.

Already they are starting to like these bankers. In fact, later, when they exchange notes, they'll come to the realization that even before the handoff, they had independently come to the conclusion that they would like to do business with this particular team.

David is now rolling into the first exhibit (the first slide). Before he asks the insurance people to turn to the first page he tells them the business message on that page, and how it ties to the theme. Only then does he ask them to open the book to page one. When they do, they experience a learning principle psychologists call *reinforcement*. In addition, they subconsciously acknowledge that David is in charge of his "presentation" (again, read *conversation*) and that the presentation is not in charge of him. He continues to roll into each exhibit. When he's done, he simply closes his book and stops talking. At this point, right on cue, the second managing director, who has said nothing yet, suddenly kicks in and, with no presentation materials or props of any kind, drives hard to the finish. He says something like, "It all comes down to this . . ." and immediately refers back to the message his associate had begun with 20 minutes earlier, recapping important highlights and ends with, "So where do we go from here? That's a question you are going to have to ask yourselves, but here's what we think makes sense." Then he outlines a brief action plan. When he stops, he looks at them and asks, "What do you think?"

Chances are, the clients are thinking, "These guys are good."

Interestingly, the "conversation" has been so crisp and answers the insurers' needs so thoroughly that they ask not a single question. Better yet, the whole thing takes less than 18 minutes. So now the only questions are aimed at how to best implement a plan to proceed.

It is only later, after the meeting, that the clients receive the complete document of the presentation, the one they never saw on the conference table. This document is a handout loaded with word slides and scores of charts. It's almost as fat and heavy as the Chicago phone book I mentioned earlier. But this document is only that—it's the official hard copy (also made available digitally) that the clients never saw nor heard. It exists for institutional and informational purposes only and to help with questions and answers, if necessary.

Preparation for this meeting takes less than 2 hours. The point is that in the world of high-stakes communication, minimal effort can produce maximal results. With a prize such as this valued at roughly $15 million, that calculates to about $7.5 million an hour, or about $125,000 a minute.

17

UP TO SPEED: FUZZBALLS AND HARDBALLS

I attended a conference where all the speakers were senior corporate officers in brand-name companies. Outside of talking too long, they shared one characteristic: Each spoke in corporate language. No one questioned their competence. But if they had hoped to be recognized as leaders in their industries, you wouldn't know it from their choice of words.

Leaders speak simply. Instead, what I got at this conference was corporate people going out of their way to sound corporate. For example, one automotive executive told the audience: "MIS is being redesigned to enhance productivity, realign interdiscipline functions, accelerate interface vis-à-vis manufacturing and the customer base, and redeploy personnel to multifunctional assignments, thereby increasing measurable productivities at the departmental level."

What this car guy was trying to say—or should have been saying—might go something like this:

"We've redesigned our computer system—getting rid of the mainframes and giving everybody a desktop and a laptop. We've launched a new satellite internal web that lets us talk to our partners in China in real time 24 hours a day. It's a far more efficient approach. Now we can do more with less, which means we can free up more of our people for global marketing and customer service."

That's what I call a *hardball*. Hardballs are specific: mainframe, satellite web, laptops, desktops, China—and most important of all, common, everyday language.

The car guy motored on: ". . . redundant design implementation to grow market share and seek appropriate growth opportunities to achieve competitive advantage via synergistic acquisitions."

These are what I call *fuzzballs*. They're squishy, vague, imprecise, insipid, and forgettable.

I look around. The man on my right is sitting upright, but his eyes are closed. He starts to lean. I nudge him. He wakes up and sits up. I feel badly for the car guy, but he doesn't look up long enough from the lectern to realize people are starting to nod off.

After a break, another speaker, the vice president of marketing of a midsize technology company, is bloviating with one fat fuzzball after another. Now he is sermonizing about how "we must redefine our eclectic market niche and prioritize significant research initiatives to impact sales and distribution mandates relative to viable alternative methodologies still under development and prior to actual executive initiative."

Which, translated into hardball, might mean: "Before we develop new products, we've got to know who is going to buy them."

Or this: "We tried—but failed—to get a foothold in the pocket pager market for medical doctors. But before we take another crack at that market, we've got to do more market research. Right now our initial research tells us that the device will sell well to home care workers, nurses, and emergency medical technicians."

The next speaker, a senior financial officer from another high-tech firm, seems to pick up where the last one leaves off. It's getting tough to tell these guys apart.

"Insofar as periods of downward pressure can be anticipated," the finance guy is fuzzballing, "preliminary projections would suggest that incremental revenue assumptions of a year ago are still contraindicated by market imbalances relative to unforeseen end-user variables such as dollar fluctuation and residual recessionary influences."

This is as good an Alan Greenspan imitation I think I have ever heard.

The man on my right is tipping into me again. I push him away. He sits bolt upright, eyes wide open.

A hardball translation of what the financial officer was trying to say might go something like this:

"We're still in a difficult market, and all indicators suggest it's not going to improve any time soon." Of course, if the finance guy is deliberately trying to obfuscate, then he's doing a great job. But I'm assuming he's trying to clarify.

Over the next two days we hear one fuzzball after another. Here are a few, with their translations:

Fuzzball: "Implement strategic initiatives to grow market share and interface corporate disciplines."

Hardball: "We've got a six-month jump on the competition with our new color document processor, the PV-100. So we're moving quickly to slash introductory prices, set up distribution in China and India, launch promotional golf and tennis marketing deals with our IBM partners, advertise heavily during the Winter

Olympics, and work closely with people from our factory in Taiwan to coordinate manufacturing and distribution."

Fuzzball: "We will enhance profitability through productivity gains achieved by reengineering quality-driven processes at the organizational level."

Hardball: "We're putting design, engineering, marketing, and customer service under one roof to make sure our customers get what they want. We expect this change will speed IMX software and first-stage Wizard processors to market in half the time and slash returns by 80 percent. Engineering and marketing will team up to design TST parallel processing extenders. These innovations have boosted revenues almost 10 percent in the first year alone."

Fuzzball: "It is imperative that we interface human capital with process reengineering to implement an environment of continuous improvement."

Hardball: "Three years ago we were like a Lexus sitting in the driveway with no tires. We had a great product, but we couldn't keep up with demand. So we set up swat teams to solve problems, added a factory, and hired more engineers. A year later we had the wheels back on the Lexus, and last year we got the car back on the road. This year, we're trying to figure out how to make it fly."

Sometimes, as you can see, the better way may be a little longer. But it's always better to sacrifice brevity for color and clarity.

> If you're an engineer, don't talk like an engineer; if you're an accountant, don't talk like an accountant.

The moral of this story is reject the arcane language of your discipline, whatever it may be. If you're an engineer, don't talk like an engineer. If you're an accountant, don't talk like an accountant. If you're a lawyer, don't talk like a lawyer. If you're a businessperson—

well, you get the idea. Trust in the ordinary language you grew up with (with the exception of serious grammatical errors), and you'll never have to worry again about how you're doing. People want an excuse to like you, and there's no better way to make that happen than to talk straight.

STAYING AHEAD OF THE PACK: THE 8-SECOND RULE AND 18-MINUTE WALL

In addition to mastering the POWER formula and the foundation, the articulate executive should also observe and faithfully practice the following fundamentals:

THE 8-SECOND RULE

The 8-second rule says that audiences will decide within 8 seconds whether you are worth listening to in the first place. This is why opening amenities are opening inanities. And this is where the P in the POWER formula comes in. The POWER formula gives you a variety of choices to start strongly.

For example, don't say, "Good morning, it's a pleasure to be here today. Today I'd like to talk about our sales outlook." You may hear a lot of people begin that way, but you can do better.

Instead, why not say something like, "This year will be our greatest ever. With just two months to go, sales in Mexico and Canada are already more than 125 percent over the same time last year, and if this growth continues, the numbers are looking even better for next year."

Instead of, "Today I would like to discuss the committee recommendations surrounding the question of contractual liabilities relative to purchasing agreements within the manufacturing group," why not try: "We've taken a hard look at contractual costs across the board—and starting today we're launching a plan to save more than $60 million a year in the manufacturing group alone."

Instead of, "I am pleased to have this opportunity to attempt to provide an assessment of developments leading up to the recent rebound in the building materials industry in the aftermath of the recession and in the current environment of ongoing record-low interest rates," how about: "Right now the housing market is red hot. More people are building or remodeling more homes today than at any time in the last half century. So it's no surprise that the building materials industry is having its biggest year ever—and we're right out in front of the wave."

These examples all begin with the ending. But you could start in other ways, by opening with a personal story, for instance. Using the housing market example, you could try something like this:

"My wife and I were on our way to dinner in a nice neighborhood in Greenwich, Connecticut, the other day when she pointed out that 11 homes on one street alone were either brand new or completely renovated in the neighborhood. And that's only the high end. The middle and low end of the real estate market are seeing the same boom in renovating and new building starts."

Or you might try an anecdote:

"Last week, officials in Palo Alto, California, announced that this will mark the third year of record new home building and renovations in a row. And Palo Alto is just one of 2,600 municipalities around the

United States reporting the hottest home building market in the last half century."

Or a rhetorical question:

"What do you think is the biggest surprise in the U.S. economy this year? The biggest surprise is that interest rates stayed historically low for the fifth year in a row, and it was the housing market—not manufacturing or financial services or even defense spending—that kept the economy afloat through the recent recession."

Or a quote:

"Fed Chairman Alan Greenspan said last week that the unexpectedly robust housing market has almost single-handedly kept the U.S. economy above water for the past three years."

Or project into the future:

"If the current red hot housing market continues to grow at present rates over the next 18 months, that will represent the longest sustained consistently outperforming housing market ever."

Or look into the past:

"Years ago, right after 9/11, housing starts in West Palm Beach, Florida, numbered only 117. There were just 132 kitchen renovations and 85 total makeovers. The building materials market was practically dead. By contrast, this year, West Palm Beach posted 2,167 housing starts, 11,502 kitchen renovations, and 1,168 total makeovers. Suppliers are running full throttle just trying to keep up with demand. This story is being repeated thousands of times in towns and cities all over America."

If you still insist on starting in the conventional way ("Good morning, it's a pleasure to be here today," etc.), here's an idea: Take the amenity ("Good morning") and stick it *after* your strong start.

This might work like this: Let's say you're an energy company executive who's been asked to speak at a national resources symposium.

And let's say you're the first speaker on the agenda, and there's no introduction. You take the lectern and tell the audience:

"Three years from now our industry is going to be so different we might not even recognize it, and this is going to happen for three reasons [then you list the three reasons].

Now you throw in the amenities:

"Good morning. I'm Bob Fisher, executive vice president of Markel Energy. I'm honored to be here today, to have a chance to tell you how I think we can work together to capitalize on six opportunities in the changes I see coming."

Conversely, if you choose to lead with the amenity, there is a way not only to soften the negative effect but also show that you have a close working relationship with your sponsor, boss, client, customer, investor, or employee. You've been introduced by association president Dave Smith, and you go to the lectern.

"Good morning. It's a pleasure and an honor to be here today," you begin, "but I must say that when I played golf over the weekend with Dave, I could see yet again that his game is almost as far off as his projections."

This sounds high risk, but actually it's not. This good-natured fun fosters the concept of camaraderie and teamwork without having to come right out and say it. The story speaks for itself. And it's funny, so it will certainly get a laugh.

Now pretend you're a human resources executive who's been asked to speak at a convention of your industry association. After you've been introduced, you take the lectern and tell the audience:

"We all have moments in our jobs that we can never forget. I experienced one of those moments the other night. I got a call from a manager we had let go in a downsizing just last year. He was polite, and I listened. He hadn't found work, he couldn't cover his children's college tuition, he had used up his savings, his wife had left him, and now he was sitting on the other end of the phone with a gun in his hand, threatening to take his own life." (The story goes on to reveal that you managed to persuade the man to put the gun away and keep trying, but the experience has left an emotional scar.)

The audience is riveted. At this point you could forge on with your message of what you perceive to be needed policy and professional changes to try to avoid similar near tragedies in the future. Or, after the story, you could pause for an amenity, maybe like this:

"I'm honored to be here with so many distinguished leaders in our field and delighted to share with you some thoughts on how I think we can work together to help avoid future near tragedies like the one I've just described." Given a choice, I would abandon opening amenities altogether. One strong start is worth a dozen amenities.

> **Experience tells us that most people tune out after 18 minutes.**

THE 18-MINUTE WALL

The 18-minute wall is an invisible barrier that can come between you and your audience. Years of experience tell us that most people tune out after 18 minutes. So what to do about the 45-minute pitch? The full answer to this question is in *The Articulate Executive*. Here's the short answer on how to break up the long presentation:

1. Have two or three presenters.
2. Throw in a DVD or video, maybe with music or voiceover.
3. Tell one anecdote or story after another to make your point (and you can talk almost as long as you like).
4. Mix in questions to your audience and/or speak for 15 minutes and devote the next half hour to questions and answers.

The important thing to remember is that even when we're at our best, we're never so good that people will want us to tie them up longer than we have to. Every leader's job is to generate guidelines that create efficiencies, cut costs, produce profits, align interests, and raise the bar. The great leader accomplishes these objectives with economy.

19

ON THE INSIDE TRACK: LEADING BY EXAMPLE

If you want action, it's always better to tell people a story than to tell them what to do. If you dictate, people may respond with their heads. But if you lead by telling a story, people will respond with their hearts.

Nothing works like anecdotes, illustrations, examples, analogies, and parables. Even fables get people thinking. Once they start thinking, they can decide for themselves to get behind the cause, adopt a new approach, or take action.

This is why it's true that one picture really can be worth 1,000 words—even if you're just painting a picture in the mind.

The most obvious historical example in Western literature is Jesus, who never wrote down a single word of teaching, according to scholars. On the other hand, the Apostle Paul wrote letters to the Ephesians, Corinthians, and Romans that expounded on the virtues of love, redemption, forgiveness, and salvation—and that's the only reason we have any idea what Paul ever had to say about anything.

Paul wrote in abstractions. Jesus spoke in parables. Which do we remember?

The point is, stories not only make things happen, they also endure.

Smart leaders understand that a little story can go a long way. When onetime PepsiCo president Chris Sinclair spoke at a senior management conference, his message was that we are all capable of more than we think. To make the point, he told a story about a 12-year-old boy growing up in India.

> **Smart leaders understand that a little story can go a long way.**

"This boy had a little bout with polio," Sinclair told his listeners. "His life was never threatened, but he did face the real possibility of spending his life in a wheelchair.

"Well, as you can imagine, at first the boy was very upset. He couldn't accept the fact that all his friends were out playing and going to school, and there he was standing on a beach and trying to learn how to walk.

"But after a while . . . gradually . . . he stopped feeling sorry for himself.

"And he concluded that while his legs wouldn't move, the real problem was in his head."

"Well, he made up his mind that within one year he wouldn't be just walking—he'd be running. And you know what? It happened."

"I know—because I was that little boy."

They got the point.

I heard the same kind of message driven home by a corporate vice president welcoming a room full of new hires to their first week on the job. He was telling them about an inspiring moment he experienced as a freshman in college when his classics professor started the school year with a little story about Socrates.

"A boy asked Socrates to teach him all he knew. Socrates took the student to a river and pushed him underwater. The boy thrashed, and when Socrates finally let him up for air, the boy demanded to know what Socrates thought he was doing. Socrates told the boy that when he wanted to learn as badly as he wanted to breathe, he would learn."

Years later, one of the former recruits told me that the story made such an impression it inspired him to go on to law school. In fact, he said he told the same story himself when he was sent to recruit graduate students at Columbia Business School.

Want your people to take responsibility for their own jobs?

The CEO of an advertising company tells a meeting of his workforce that leadership emerges from absolute commitment to the job and the company. To make the point, he talks about how W. L. Gore & Associates, maker of Gore-Tex, a high-tech sports fabric, grooms leaders.

The CEO tells his audience how Gore always insists that "we don't manage people here." No fancy titles. No official authority. No real bosses. A machine operator, for example, gets tired of his job and wants to try something else. He transfers to product development, soon engineers a new product, and winds up manager for the new product line. That's the kind of associate, Gore says, who not only contributes to the enterprise but also likes responsibility—the kind of person who rises naturally to leadership.

At a time when a frenzy of talent poaching was sweeping Silicon Valley, a harried company cofounder from South Africa assembles his employees to make the point that a lot of people are wasting time trying desperately to find what they've already got.

"When I was a kid in South Africa," he tells them, "I heard a story about a miner who quit his job and home to go off and find his own diamond mine, but it wasn't until he returned home after two fruitless years the he finally found his diamonds—in his own back yard." He continues: "A few months ago we saw a few miners of our own head out the door. Most of them have already returned, and we're glad to have them back."

He went on to talk about loyalty, teamwork, and a common sense of purpose. Not everybody bought the message, but defections plunged 80 percent.

Fed up with stupid Mickey Mouse regulations? A frustrated senior manager takes the stage to caution against overzealous rules that threaten productivity. He tells how one of his own engineers needs a simple battery replacement but discovers that in a new push to cut costs the company will no longer supply batteries. The engineer races to a nearby store, buys his battery and finishes his project on time. He submits an expense voucher for $3.84 for the new battery plus $2.25 for use of his own car. The voucher goes out in triplicate and the department's controller calculates that in the end the battery winds up costing $30 in processing expenses plus an undetermined amount in lost productivity.

The dumb rule is dropped, and the company overhauls its entire cost-savings program.

The CEO of a rapidly growing services company tells an audience how he personally manages damage control when customers complain of ignorant and indifferent receptionists. He tells how he sends the corporate jet around the country to pick up division receptionists and treats them to a two-day seminar at corporate headquarters. He greets the receptionists himself. They are made to understand the importance of their jobs, lodged in good hotels, and after each day's work, taken to fine restaurants.

The personal attention pays off. Customers stop complaining, and now the CEO says he hears only compliments about his receptionists— and business has never been better.

Want to get people to think outside the box and keep it simple?

At a symposium on innovation, a guest speaker tells a story about how Thomas Edison selected the best engineers for his projects. The great inventor handed job applicants a light bulb and asked them how much water it would hold.

Most applicants spent hours trying to figure the bulb's interior space with complex calculations. But a few simply filled the bulb with water and then poured the water into a measuring cup.

Edison always hired the engineers who kept it simple.

The lesson is not lost on the listeners, who are all design engineers.

A recent corporate conference features a quality-control expert who argues that to achieve true quality, we should all approach quality as if our jobs, and even our lives, depend on it. He offers an anecdote that gets everybody's attention. The Air Force, he tells them, has a policy that people who pack parachutes periodically have to make jumps themselves. The Air Force, he points out, does not have a quality-control problem with chute packing.

In the spirit of trying to instill trust and confidence in a company with a shaky history of labor relations, a new division head tells his salaried workers that from now on, as just one example of good faith, the facility will start running its cafeteria on the honor system. No more locks on the sandwich and soft drink machines, no cash registers, and no cashiers—just an open cash box.

His gamble pays off. The workers repay the gesture of respect with respect. A year later, the vice president tells his management team at headquarters that they've not had a single shortfall and that in a typical day the cash box will be filled with well over $200.

The open policy is embraced as a best practice and introduced into other corporate facilities, where management sees similar positive results. Curiously, they also note that since the plan's inception, sick days are down and productivity is up.

Since the beginning of recorded history, leaders have recognized not just the value but the actual necessity of telling stories to spur change and inspire innovation. This is no less true in business. That's why the most successful change makers in every industry already know that if you want action, it's always better to tell people a story than to tell them what to do.

STAYING AHEAD: HOW TO LEVERAGE THE LANGUAGE

Unfortunate but true: A decision on whether to enlist your service, buy your product, or hire you or fire you could depend on just one word.

Many people are unaware that a majority of decision makers put a premium on good grammar, a rich working vocabulary, and confident articulation. With a noticeable drop in grammatical standards in recent years and little practice of eloquence in the workplace, these valuable attributes are becoming less common and therefore more prized.

Which, of course, opens opportunities.

Thousands of times every day salespeople don't get the order and managers don't get the assignment. And those otherwise able professionals may never know why—because the decision makers will never tell them.

The reason things can go wrong is because after just one or two tiny grammatical slips, the decision maker may get the incorrect perception that the person on the far side of the table or desk, on the other end of the phone, or popping up as an e-mail has an incomplete education.

Geniuses, brilliant entrepreneurs, and other wizards aside, no boss, no decision maker, and no potential client or customer wants to believe that the person they are supposed to be hiring, or assigning, or doing business with has an incomplete education.

For example, a boss may feel reluctant to put such a manager in front of a board or a new client, at the head of a negotiating team, or even on a golf course playing a round with an important prospective customer.

This is a shame because that very person may be just the right one for the assignment—by any other measurement.

And yet that person *still* won't get the chance simply because of a little word here and there that happens to get in the way.

This is a problem not often discussed or even recognized. It can hurt customer relations, productivity, morale, and ultimately, revenues. Every responsible decision maker should be working to correct it.

Here's just one example why: A senior executive tells me that he's disappointed in one of his reports, whom he's hired as a likely replacement for himself. When I ask why, he tells me that the executive in question, an operations manager, has great organizational and managerial skills but comes across as a semi-illiterate with clients and his own employees.

In what way? I ask.

He doesn't know how to use the English language properly, the senior executive replies, and adds that he isn't entirely comfortable placing the junior officer in social and business situations where he represents the company.

The next day I get a chance to see what the senior executive is talking about.

It's the operations guy's turn to speak at a management meeting. I'm not focused on what he's saying but instead trying to listen to how he's saying it. I pick up little bits and pieces, which by themselves mean nothing. But taken together they reveal potential shortcomings which—if they are any indication of how he typically presents himself and are allowed to continue unchecked—can't bode well for his bid for the top spot.

My notes wind up looking something like this:

"We did real good. If we would have accepted the original proposal. . . . He always knows where he's at. . . . When the competition chopped prices, we got bit real bad. . . . There's floor managers that stay ahead of the load curve. . . . There's three things we can do. . . . If I was him, I'd be looking at my return on investment. . . . I asked him to come to the meeting with his boss and I. . . . Let's don't forget that the real issue is. . . ."

He's oblivious to these blips. But he's a likable guy. He seems relaxed and comfortable with his audience. You come away with the notion that he enjoys his work. And I want to believe that he's as talented as he is likable. Right now, however, I'm distracted by the blips.

I'll call this first batch the "big potatoes." In a minute I'll get to the "small potatoes." But first let's take these "big potatoes" one by one and try to turn them into *pommes de terre*:

1. "We did *real* good."
   Better: "We did *really well*."
   Why: *Real* needs an *-ly* as an adverb to modify the predicate nominative *good*. But *good* is the wrong word because *did . . . good*" means did a good thing. *Did . . . well* means what it says.
2. "If we would have accepted the original proposal. . . ."
   Better: "Had we accepted" or "If we had accepted. . . ."
   Why: "If we would have accepted" is just plain clumsy and unnecessarily complex (the grammatical explanation is a little unwieldy, too, so I'll spare you).
3. "He always knows where he's at. . . ."
   Better: "He always knows where he is. . . ."
   Why: *At* never follows *is* or *are* at the end of any sentence.

141

4. "When the competition dropped prices, we *got bit* pretty *bad*. . . ."

   Better: "When the competition dropped prices, we got *bitten* pretty *badly*."

   Why: *He bit* is fine, but *got bit* is not. *Bitten* must follow *got*. *Bad* is an adverb modifying *bit*, so you've got to throw on the *-ly*.

5. "*Don't let's* forget. . . ."

   Better: "*Let's not* forget. . . ."

   Why: You can't ask people not to do something you're asking them to do.

6. "*There's* floor managers *that* stay ahead of the load curve. . . ."

   Better: "*There are* floor managers *who* stay ahead of the load curve. . . ."

   Why: *Managers* is plural, so you've got to change *there is* to *there are*. Most times the pronoun *who* is better than *that* when you're talking about people.

7. "If I *was him*, I'd look first at my return on investment. . . ."

   Better: "If I *were* he, I'd look first at my return on investment. . . ."

   Why: The language is changing, and this one is a little tricky. Today, *were* follows *if*, and *he* or *she* should follow *were*. However, the correct form sounds a little stuffy, and in the years to come this rule probably will fade into history.

8. "I asked him to come to the meeting with his boss and I. . . ."

   Better: ". . . with his boss and *me*."

   Why: *Me, him, us*, and *them* always follow the preposition *with*.

So much for the "big potatoes." These are what I call "stealth bombs" because you'll never know you have them until they go off and the damage is already done. If you happen to be on a leadership path and these particular potatoes pop up all the time in your daily use of the language, then I'd have to say that either they go or you go. You both can't be in the same space at the same time.

To a lesser degree, this is true as well with the "small potatoes." Here are some of them.

1. "As far as quality management, we've hired some of the best people in the business. . . ."
   Better: "As far as quality management *goes*. . . ."
   Why: You've got to stick *goes* or *is concerned* after *As far as* to complete the clause.
2. "*In terms of assistance*, we will always help if they ask us to. . . ."
   Better: "We will always help if they ask us to. . . ."
   Why: *In terms of* is redundant. Ditch it.
3. "Who remembers *their* mistakes when things are going well?"
   Better: "Who remembers his mistakes. . . ."
   Why: *Who* refers to just one person.
4. "I told *her* that was *one they* said they could do for *him*, but *he* thought they were going to talk with *her* about *that* first, and that's when the confusion began." (I'll bet it did.)
   Better: "I told *Sally* that was a *project* the *accountants* said they could do for *Jim*, but *Jim* thought the *accountants* were going to talk with *Sally* about the *project* first."
   Why: The indefinite reference pronoun is confusing. If you read a paragraph, you can always refer back to the noun. But when you're listening, you can't go back and check. This is why repetition in prose is a *vice*, but when you're speaking, it's a *device*. So remember to use the noun instead of the pronoun so that your listeners don't get lost.
5. "Rita loves a challenge even more than *I*. . . ."
   Better: "Rita loves a challenge even more than *me*. . . ."

Why: You could say "... than I *do*," but if you don't, then you've got to end the sentence with *me* (as the object of *than*).

6. "This particular transaction was an adventure for both Rita and *myself* as well...."
   Better: "... for both Rita and me."
   Why: *Me* is simpler, cleaner, and less clunky. When you're talking (or writing), the simplest choice is usually the best.

7. "The partnership started to unravel when the last *hanger-ons* started heading for the exits...."
   Better: "... when the last *hangers-on* started heading for the exits...."
   Why: Weird as it sometimes may sound, the correct form places the plural on the first word, as in *attorneys general*.

8. "A large percentage of employees *are* working longer hours...."
   Better: "A large percentage of employees *is* working longer hours...."
   Why: The verb refers back to *percentage* and not to the prepositional phrase *of employees*, so the verb must be singular, not plural.

9. "I worry about these *kind* of omissions...."
   Better: "I worry about these *kinds* of omissions...."
   Why: *These* and *omissions* are plural, so *kind* must be plural, too.

10. "The contract was *a* sort of an update...."
    Better: "The contract was *sort of* an update...."
    Why: You don't need the *a*.

11. "... We've all heard that story told in various *medias*...."
    Better: ... "in various *media*...."
    Why: *Media* is already plural. You don't need the -*s*.

12. "... No one in *their* right mind believes...."
    Better: "... No one in *his* (or *her*) right mind believes...."
    Why: *No one* (not one) is singular.

13. *"Your* and *my* ideas about how to cut costs may differ. . . ."
    Better: "Your ideas about how to cut costs may differ from *mine*. . . ."
    Or: *"Your* ideas and *my* ideas about how to cut costs may differ. . . ."
    Why: For clarity, you need either to separate *you* and *my* (changed to *mine*) or throw in another *idea*.

14. ". . . These facts support *us* taking steps to. . . ."
    Better: ". . . The facts support *our* taking steps to. . . ."
    Why: As annoyingly pedantic as it may sound, *-ing* words (gerunds) require the possessive (as in *our*).

15. ". . . Every part of our business—R&D, manufacturing, operations, marketing, and finance—*need* to trim costs."
    Better: ". . . *needs* to trim costs."
    Why: *Needs* refers back to *part*, which is singular (everything between the dashes is just a supporting clause to *part*).

16. ". . . We're not going to *lay* down and play dead. . . ."
    Better: ". . . *lie* down and play dead."
    Why: You can lay an egg and lay down a spoon, but you *lie* down.

17. ". . . When Chuck *graduated* MIT. . . ."
    Better: ". . . when Chuck *graduated from* MIT. . . ."
    Why: This is a common error. You can't *graduate* MIT (even though a lot of people seem to think you can). Chuck is doing the graduating, not somehow helping MIT to graduate. So you need the *from*.

18. ". . . These three processes are *equally* as important as. . . ."
    Better: ". . . These three processes are *equal in importance to*. . . or . . . *are as* important as. . . ."
    Why: *Equally* is not only redundant but implies that the individual processes, taken separately, are equal in importance to one another as well.

19. "... We want to know what's going on *inside of* the customer's head. ..."
    Better: "... *inside* the customer's head. ..."
    Why: The *of* is clumsy and unnecessary.

20. "... Sometimes *I can't* hardly understand why. ..."
    Better: "... Sometimes I *can* hardly understand. ..."
    Why: It's bad enough when you can hardly understand something. But when you *can't* hardly understand, do you understand? Just get rid of the negative.

21. "... We have *a myriad of* obstacles ahead. ..."
    Better: "... We have *myriad* obstacles ahead. ..."
    Why: *Myriad* means "many," so *a myriad of* would be incorrect.

22. "... To decide whether or not. ..."
    Better: *Whether* already implies *or not*, so you don't need the *or not*.

23. "... We made the decision to acquire, *only* the regulators overruled us. ..."
    Better: "... We made the decision to acquire, *but* the regulators overruled us. ..."
    Why: *Only* in this context seems to make the unintended point that it was only the regulators who did the overruling.

24. "... *Being that* we expect the cost-cutting measures to produce results by the third quarter. ..."
    Better: "... *Since* we expect. ..."
    Why: Why say *being that* when you can say *since*?

25. "... That's why we have *orientated* ourselves. ..."
    Better: "... That's why we have *oriented* ourselves. ..."
    Why: The syllable *-ate* is sneaking into the language, but it's awkward, and we ought to try to keep it out.

26. "... We *don't have but* three years to reverse this trend. ..."
    Better: "... We *have but* three years to reverse this trend ..."
    or "... we have *only* three years. ..."
    Why: This is another one of those double-negative situations.
    Bag the *don't*.

These are all "small potatoes," and if you just can't shake them, you can still live with them. At the same time, I'd like to see them all go right out the window along with the "big potatoes."

English is a robust, flexible language that didn't even exist 1,500 years ago. It's a rich soup made from a colorful garden of other languages, including Latin, French, Anglo-Saxon, Gaelic, Celtic, Old Norse, and Germanic. It changes so fast that grammarians and scholars have a tough time keeping up. Some of the basic rules you learned in third grade, for example, might not be valid now. On top of that, America is so vast, whole sections of the country tend to develop regional ways of talking.

For instance, you hear more *can't hardly* and *real good* in the South and West than you do in the Northeast, and that's fine. But the point is that while regional dialect might work with regional businesses, it might not be appropriate at the national or international levels.

The rule of thumb should be that at all levels of business, ordinary, day-to-day language is preferable to corporate language and certainly a good thing. But it stops being a good thing when it starts to mangle generally accepted (not regionally accepted) grammatical standards.

That's why it's conceivable that a single inept sentence, phrase, or even the choice of a single word could eclipse competence, brainpower, and talent. It's unfair, but it's possible. And it happens.

21

HOW TO AVOID THE CRASH AND BURN

Putting PowerPoint or any other visual aids system in the hands of an amateur is not unlike putting an eight-year-old behind the wheel of a bus (to stretch the analogy off the racetrack for a moment). Not only is the driver likely to get hurt, but everybody else on the bus (team members, associates, etc.) could suffer similar setbacks by association. This is not to mention the bus itself—the corporate image—which could wind up in a ditch.

The irony is that amateurs often don't realize that they are amateurs. Worse, they sometimes see themselves as experienced pros. They rely on visual aids to a degree that invites a kind of public self-mutilation—the only instrument of torture being the misused PowerPoint itself. That very PowerPoint could be a different kind of torture for the audience. This sorry state of affairs can go largely unrecognized and unremedied for years.

Nobody gains from badly executed visual aids.

At the same time, visual aids in the hands of a talented driver can do no harm and may even do some good.

For example, let's say that a chief operating officer of a parent company with flat sales and high costs is pushing for a reorganization. He schedules a presentation for all the senior officers in the company.

He puts together something that looks like this:

SLIDE 1

Predictable, dronish corporate speak. Fairly dull and lifeless.

> **Divisional Plan Summary Data**
>
> Reorganization plus New Marketing and Strategy Initiatives as of Jan. 15 (provisional, for review by management committee)

SLIDE 2

Inane, unreadable gobbledygook in text portion. Hard to decipher because it's so small on slide. Graphic very small, hard to see, confusing.

Last Year's Revenue by Group and Quarter, Normalized for Comparison

- Broken out according to old groups (before reorganization according to plan to be subsequently reviewed)

- Normalized to a 100-point scale for comparison, and with a regression trend line for Group A overlaid (although the trend has low statistical validity)

- Note that with the exception of Group A, 3rd Quarter, revenues trend pretty much level (which is the problem we need to address) and this comparison does not reveal any significant differences between groups either

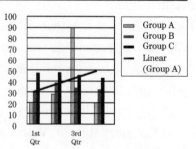

SLIDE 3

Impossible to track, too cluttered, hard to read.

Analysis of Cost Savings and Payoffs from Reorganization

	Synergy in Procurement	Cost savings from reduction in labor costs	Expected customer benefits	Overall Assessments
New Group A	Low (1–5% savings)	High if we do the downsizing in first quarter	No data yet, the customer research group's report is late	Cost savings range from low to high depending on reorganization
New Group B	High (10% or more savings)	Low, 5% or less	No data yet, the customer research group's report is late	Cost savings in mid range, 10% approx.
New Group C	Medium, 5–10% saved??	Low, 4–5% estimated	No data yet, the customer research group's report is late	Cost savings moderate, 3–5% overall?
Overall for Division	Estimated 7.25% savings	2–5%, depending on speed of implementation	See above (not my responsibility)	Est. 5.5% cost reduction, but don't have revenue data yet so can't estimate real returns

SLIDE 4

Standard word slide. Overwhelms whatever presenter is trying to say. Dwarfs key graphic, which is effectively lost.

Main Features of Reorganization Plan (Version 7b)

- Redefine groups according to industry and customer type instead of geography as they are now
- Add Coordination Officer to funnel all purchase and hiring request (which reduces waste and identifies potential synergies, see Memo on Achieving Synergy from Reorganization)

- By combining reorganization with the downsizing, we can cut redundant personnel according to Staffing Analysis Report (available on line, let me know if you need a printout copy)

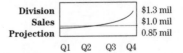

Division Sales Projection — $1.3 mil / $1.0 mil / 0.85 mil

Q1 Q2 Q3 Q4

SLIDE 5

Word slide detracts from presenter. Hard to read; offers nothing presenter could not say without slide.

Main Features of Reorganization Plan (Version 7b)

- Also affects structure of sales and marketing groups, which will have to be realigned according to new territories. Specialists to focus on industries and work in teams.

- We're awaiting the projections for revenue by group for the new marketing/sales groups, but we expect there to be significant growth in sales resulting from focusing on industries and drawing specialists from each of the old div. Sales forces to make new industry teams

- Purchasing / procurement can be done centrally for all of the new groups, out of division HQs

- Group A to focus on manufacturers, Group B on the Insurance and Banking Industries, Group C to handle Government and Other (small business, etc. etc.)

SLIDE 6

More of the same.

Main Features of Reorganization Plan (Version 7b)

- Sales will probably drop in first quarter during transition, but grow to exceed current level by middle of year (see graph, previous slide)

- Add Coordination Officer to funnel all purchase and hiring request (which reduces waste and identifies potential synergies, see Memo on Achieving Synergy from Reorganization)

- By combining reorganization with the downsizing, we can cut redundant personnel according to Staffing Analysis Report (available on line, let me know if you need a printout copy)

- Purchasing / procurement can be done centrally for all of the new groups, out of division HQs

SLIDE 7

Word slide hard to read. If anywhere, summary belongs at top of presentation. More of a problem here than a solution.

Summary of Proposal

- Pending final report from Sales & Marketing Reorganization Subcommittee, but expect sales to drop at first, then recover and exceed last year's levels by a significant amount
- By combining downsizing of workforce with reorganization of all the groups at one time, we make the transition quicker and achieve more synergies on the cost side according to our analysis
- The main areas where synergies can be expected to generate significant (from low to high, see table with analysis in earlier slide) cost savings are:
- Procurement (purchasing, logistics, etc. etc.)
- Sales and marketing (which by specializing according to customer type instead of geographically will be more effective and able to offer more customer benefits, making our offerings more competitive) will be reorganized to specialize by customer type
- The biggest impact will be from cutting labor force by approx. 7% across the board (but Group C will get the deepest cuts because they have a number of previously-independent, now redundant, functions)

- **Any Questions?**

- (Let me know if you need copies of theses slides or where to go to download them for further review during your decision-making process)

Seen this one before? Chances are you have, or something very much like it. And therein lies the rub—because this common misuse of PowerPoint accomplishes, paradoxically, the opposite of what it is intended to do, which is to help clarify a message. If fact, this presentation only obfuscates.

To make matters worse, our friend the COO is using this wordy concoction as his notes. So he's trying to paraphrase or read verbatim every sentence, which only serves to make him look unprepared and not nearly as bright as he actually is (if he really knew what he was talking about, couldn't he just talk about it?).

The good news is that it's only seven slides. The bad news is that in this example we have used only seven slides to try to make a point as quickly as possible. It is very likely that our COO actually might have come armed with as many as 50 similar slides. This exacerbating effect, of course would serve only to severely try the patience of his audience, probably muddy the communication further, and ultimately drive his chances for enrollment down to near zero.

We'll call this a worst-case scenario.

A better case might look something like this:

SLIDE 1

Summary

- **Sales growth**
- Quicker transition
- More synergies = more cost savings
- Sales and marketing reorganized by customer type
- Other functions centralized at Division HQs
- **Cut payroll 7%**

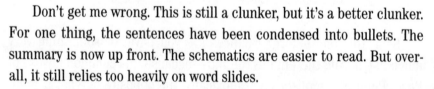

Don't get me wrong. This is still a clunker, but it's a better clunker. For one thing, the sentences have been condensed into bullets. The summary is now up front. The schematics are easier to read. But overall, it still relies too heavily on word slides.

An even better case scenario might look like this:

SLIDE 1
New corporate logo.

SLIDE 2

New Plan Pays Off in 6 Months

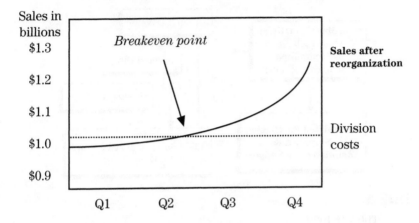

SLIDE 3

The New Organization

- Group A: Manufacturers

- Group B: Insurance and Banking Industries

- Group C: Government and Small Business

SLIDE 4

Organizational Structure

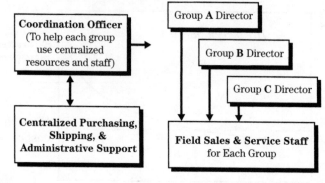

SLIDE 5
New corporate logo.

Not bad. Now, instead of a word slide, we've got the COO presenting a new logo along with his plan, which gets everybody's attention. He deliberately seizes the opening moments to focus the audience's attention on himself and what he is saying and to press his case from the outset without having to compete with his own word slides. The "summary" bullets we saw in the last scenario are now folded into this opening monologue (but not shown on the screen). In the course of pressing his case, he introduces the proposed new logo. After that, he's showing only three slides. Then it's back to the logo slide and a hard drive to the finish, leaving them, we hope, enthused and enrolled.

Can it be better yet? I think so:

SLIDE 1
New corporate logo.

SLIDE 2

6 Month Payoff

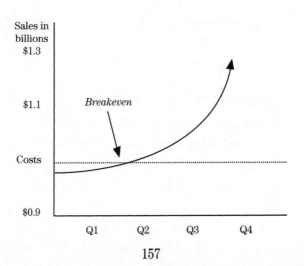

SLIDE 3

This slide would follow a contrasting slide of what the organization used to look like.

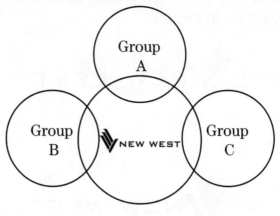

SLIDE 4

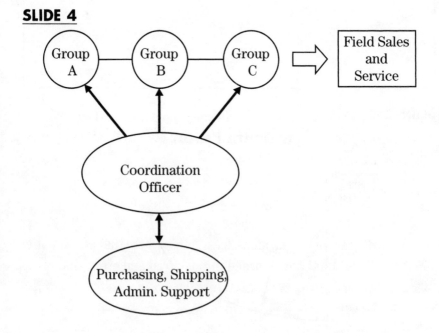

SLIDE 5
New corporate logo.

Now here's the best of all:

ZERO SLIDES

Before you howl in protest—and some people would—I must amend this postulation with conditions. I have said many times that the greatest leaders—including business leaders—don't use slides. This is true in part because they are in fact the leaders, and when they talk, people listen. That's why people listened to the Pope—even though what he said was virtually unintelligible at times.

Leaders, with some exceptions, have gotten where they are only after years of talking. Many have learned through trial and error what works and what doesn't. Most have noticed that the closer you get to the top of organizations, the more slides seem to disappear.

So by the time they finally take their seats in the corner office, they are comfortable working without crutches or props of any kind. (With the exception of periodic board meetings, in which case the visuals are prepared in accordance with some ancient formula dating back to 1950 by a junior person on the third floor.)

However, if you are not yet CEO or don't expect to be anytime soon, in order to do what the CEO does and simply forego slides altogether (and at the same time gather the same kind of eclat that the CEO enjoys), you must

1. Be passionate about your subject.
2. Know your stuff cold.
3. Adhere unflinchingly to the fundamentals: strong start, one theme, great examples, ordinary language, and strong ending.
4. Understand your audience.
5. Be comfortable with yourself.
6. Be prepared to tell personal stories, recall anecdotes, ask questions, project into the future, draw contrast to the past— all to advance your message or cause.
7. Walk the stage without benefit of notes, outline, lectern, or slides.
8. Talk no more than 18 minutes (unless you have lots and lots of great stories to tell to make your point; you share the stage with someone else; you throw in DVDs, CDs, or videotapes; or break up your talk with questions).

For those of you who despair at the thought of a presentation with just a handful of slides or can't conceive of a presentation with no slides at all, there is hope. Here it is: *Your word slides never go away*! Even though you may show only three slides on the wall behind you or actually have the courage to venture forth into the pioneering territory of no slides at all, *you will always have your hard copy, which will become the document.* Now the document doesn't have to look or sound anything like what you put on the wall. So if you find it hard to part with endless word slides and thousands of bullets and sentences, take comfort in the knowledge that someone may actually be reading that hefty tome right now on the way back home on the plane. (We would have to assume in this case that she somehow missed your live presentation.)

Finally, a brief reminder:

1. Start and end each presentation with just you doing the talking (no slides other than perhaps a logo).
2. Stick all slides in the middle.
3. Introduce each new slide while the old slide is still up.

The greatest risk that you will crash and burn lies not with you, but with your slides. So beware your buddy who tells you that you don't have enough slides (show him the thick document with all the extra charts and data and words that you intend to hand out afterwards—and remind him you've got plenty of time left over for questions and answers).

The golden rule is to use slides the way you would a controlled substance—a little can go a long way and do some good, but too much can kill.

THE LAST LAP

 Have you looked around lately—I mean really looked?

Chances are you will notice, among other things, that you've got a menacing phalanx of steely-eyed competitors looking to give you a hot run for your money. Most are probably ambitious, committed, tireless, and focused—just like you—and some may even be as smart and talented. You also may be getting the feeling that those competitors are gaining ground and proliferating like rabbits. You may be asking yourself where did all these people suddenly come from?

The fact is that while we were all having lunch, the world turned. In the blink of an eye—just about the time we were putting down that empty cup of decaf and patting our lips with the napkin—things got tougher and more complicated. The playing field got crowded. The race speeded up. Customers demanded more. An epidemic of lying, cheating, and ferocious greed broke out. Regulators cracked down. Senior corporate officers and analysts went to jail. Processes became even more so-phisticated. Cost cutting became a religion. Companies imploded. Whole levels of management disappeared. People started working longer hours, taking shorter vacations, and grinding weekends and nights. It was—and is—a case of too many people competing for too few dollars and a dwindling pile of resources.

In every developed country, business activity got up to speed and raced down the track, and in places such as India and China, the speed-ometer spiked straight into the red zone. This all came to pass while we were having lunch.

We were all caught a little off guard—and that's why this book matters.

The question that counts is: Where does this new reality put you? Anyone taking even a cursory look at their industry who doesn't see the potholes and obstacles is asleep at the wheel and headed for a wreck.

So what can you do? How can you differentiate yourself and your business right now in the eyes of customers, shareholders, and employ-ees? You can make a better product cheaper, but that takes research and development money and time. Or you can give better customer ser-vice. But in a skeptical world, that effort may flounder for a year or two until customers finally decide that you're serious. You could throw in more incentives and lots of marketing bells and whistles, but you know that in the long run that won't do it either.

The answer is simple and doesn't cost a penny (unless you invest in a professional like myself—and even then the cost is only incremental compared with the payback). The answer is—starting today—you can put to immediate and profitable use all the guidance and tips you have harvested from this book and *The Articulate Executive*. The race you are in is congested with competitors who would like nothing more than to leave you in their rear-view mirrors. The race is on with customers who deal with 25 other vendors every day, with employees who need constant inspiration and direction, with shareholders and investors craving guidance and looking for signs of intelligent life in their managements, with reporters who can put you on the map (if handled with care), and with vast industry audiences who haven't heard a good business speaker in five years.

You must do something immediately to dodge getting lost in that thundering pack of smart people jockeying for daylight all around you. Obviously, the first thing you do is get in the race. To get in the race, first you've got to seize the passion. If you can't bring yourself to get excited about your company, product or service, then at least throw yourself into the competition itself. While you're gearing yourself up for action and your mind is quietly putting things into sharp focus, go ahead and let your heart race a little. Now you can begin to turn yourself into an instrument of leadership. So load up your tool bag and go to work. Get out of the office, down on the floor, and out into the field. Roll up your sleeves and start talking to your peers, team members, employees, customers, decision makers, investors, shareholders, board members, and anyone and everyone who can help you present your case and win your race.

Your mission is to pump up performance, prime productivity, and push profitability. Your partners are your people, customers, and shareholders. Your job is to connect. Your objective is constant improvement across the board at every level of your business. But if any of these things are to happen, you must act. A plan, idea, even a vision by itself is not enough to make you get where you want to go. Good intentions, even a knowledge of the game, will get you nowhere.

You must act. You must become the articulate executive in action. You must do it for yourself, your company, and even your country. And let's not forget your family and friends, who are up there somewhere in the gallery, cheering their hearts out as you disappear with the pack around the first bend.

CHECKLIST

For 25 years, people have been saying to me, "I wish I had learned this when I first started my career," or "They never taught this to us in business school," or "Where were you when I needed you?"

This is why I'm giving you a simple little checklist from *The Articulate Executive* and *The Articulate Executive in Action*. You need only flip to the back of this book when you need a quick snapshot refresher on how to play like a pro.

Here's the checklist:

- Forget opening amenities. If you must use them, throw them in only after a strong start.
- Remember POWER—*P* Punch strong start, *O* One theme, *W* Windows/examples, *E* Ear/ordinary language, *R* Retention/strong ending.
- Begin every presentation without slides (unless it's a blue or black blank, title, logo, video, or montage).

- End every presentation without slides (return to logo or blank, etc.).
- Skip word slides in the actual presentation itself, but save them for the handout or official document (hard copy or digital).
- Instead of word slides, use only charts, tables, schematics, and photos.
- If you must use word slides, use only brief quotes, lists of products or people; and instead of bullets use just one word or phrase, such as a large centerpiece banner in the middle of each slide. Limit banner words to one slide each.
- Stick your slides in the middle of your presentation.
- Avoid white backgrounds, and go easy on the pastel colors.
- Make slides simple—make them complex only when complexity is the point you want to make.
- Use just one image per slide (unless you're preparing a presentation book).
- Presentation books should be thin. The handout document can be as fat as you want it to be.

EXECUTION

- Roll into the next slide while the old slide is still up (an eight-second intro to the business point of the next slide).
- Click to the next slide only after you've finished the roll-in.
- Operate in the GO ZONE—audience eye level. OZONE is too high. NO ZONE is too low.
- Don't hand out hard copy ahead of time—unless the client or customer insists.
- Distribute hard copy only after the presentation.

- In team presentations, take care of the housekeeping—such as introductions—before you sit down at the table.
- In sit-down presentations, use silent clues (no intros) to achieve seamless transitions from one presenter to the next.
- If you use a lectern, step back far enough (maybe two to three inches) so you can keep your head up. Let your eyes do all the work (checking your text, notes, or outline).
- If you use a prepared text, use upper and lowercase, enlarge the words, double space, make every sentence a separate paragraph, don't track sentences to the top of the next page (finish your last sentence on the same page), and put numbers in all four corners.

This is a sample of the format, actual size and type-face you should use in any prepared text speech which you intend to deliver word for word.

- Remember—it's UP-down-UP with your eyes, not down-UP-down.
- Breathe a lot—especially between sentences.
- Practice pausing for effect.
- When you're finished, try asking, "What do you think?"

RULES

- Live by the eight-second rule: Audiences will decide within eight seconds if you're worth listening to.
- Respect the 18-minute wall: Audiences will tune out if you go beyond this psychological barrier. [If you must go longer, include another speaker, show a videotape, tell relevant stories (anecdotes), and throw in more Q&A.]
- If you can't define your theme in eight seconds, either you don't have a message, or you don't know it.

DRESS

- Keep it simple. Keep it conservative. Invest in quality.

STAGE FRIGHT

- If you think less about yourself and how you're doing and more about your message and how it's going to help the people you're talking to, you may never have to worry again about how you're doing.

OTHER TIPS

- Be prepared.
- Think of your audience as family and friends.
- Imagine those times you thought you did well.
- Remember that it always feels worse than it looks.

This checklist is intentionally basic and minimalist. It won't make you a superstar, but at the very least it can help you to prevent avoidable errors, bad habits, and self-inflected wounds. It can put anyone ahead of the competition and give even the tortoises among us a fair shot at the finish.

INDEX

Absentmindedness, 37

Amenity, 129–131, 167

Analogy, 133

Anecdote, 128–129, 133

Arcane language, 124

Art of the Deal, The (Trump), 86

Articulate Executive - Learn to Look, Act, and Sound Like a Leader (Toogood), 27, 28, 50, 131, 164, 167

Artifice, 36

Attention-getting presentation, 98–99, 115–119

Attention-getting techniques, 128–129

Audience, 23–24

Authenticity, 89–91

Author (Toogood), 178

Autonomous rule, 104

Beers, Charlotte, 5

Bethune, Gordon, 64

Big potatoes, 141–142

bin Laden, Osama, 16

Blather, 38

Bogle, John, 72

Boneheaded egocentrics, 101–102

Boorishness, 38

Boredom, 19–21

Bottom line, 57–61, 115–117

Business likability, 89–94

Candor, 36

Cautionary tale (cutting costs), 77–81

Character, 37

Checklist, 167–171

   dress, 170

   execution, 168–169

other tips, 170–171
rules, 170
stage fright, 170
Choice of words, 53–56, 121–125
Christ, Jesus, 17
Churchill, Winston, 51
Civility, 38
Clarity, 36
Cohesion, 38
Color, 37
Communication, 58
Communications value added (CVA),
    7–17
  boredom, 19–21
  darks side of, 15–16
  global perspective, 10
  goal setting, 10
  know your audience, 23–24
  master of your presentation, 22
  passion, 10
  preparation, 25
  principles, 19–25
  talk about what you know, 22–23
  talk in pictures, 24–25
  value added, 21–22
  what is it, 15
Competence, 37
Concentration, 37
Concept, 36
Conflict management, 101–107
Confusing, 38
Consistency, 38, 91
Continental Airlines, 64
Continuity, 38
Conversation vs. lecture/presentation,
    111–119
Conviction, 36
Coolness, 37
Corporate robo-speak, 53, 121–125

Corporate scandals, 15–16
Cost cutting, 77–81
Creativity, 39, 83–88
Credibility, 36
Crispness, 37–38
Cutting costs (cautionary tale), 77–
    81
CVA. *See* Communications value added
    (CVA)

Departmental rivalries, 101–107
Doubt, 36
Dr. Jekyll and Mr. Hyde analogy, 89–91
Drabness, 37
Dress (attire), 170

Ebbers, Bernie, 15–16
Edison, Thomas, 137
Ego-based rivalries, 101–107
8-second rule, 127–131
18-minute wall, 131
Elizabeth I, 50
Emptiness, 36
Execution, 168–169

Fable, 133
Fast start, 57–61, 115–117
Fastow, Andrew, 16
Fear, 37
50 percent problem, 41
50 percent solution, 41–45
Finley, Timothy, 63
Forbes, Steve, 93
Foundation, 111–112
Fuzzball, 53–56, 121–125
Fuzziness, 36

Gates, Bill, 63, 93
Gerster, Lou, 66

Getting right down to business, 57–61, 115–117
Ghandi, Mahatma, 17
Glass, David, 69
Goal setting, 10
Grammar, 139–147
Greenspan, Alan, 54

Haldeman, Ed, 72
Hard-copy handout, 58, 168
Hardball, 53–56, 121–125
Health South, 16
Henry, Patrick, 51
Hewlett, Bill, 71
Hi-C's, 35–39
Hiam, Alex, 102, 104, 106
Hitler, Adolf, 16
Hussein, Saddam, 16

Iacocca, Lee, 8
IBM, 66
Immelt, Jeff, 9–11, 35
in-depth, 31
Incompetence, 37
Indifference, 4
Information, 58
Innovation, 73–76
Internal damage control, 105
Intracorporate rivalry (hostility), 101–107

Jones, Bob, 16

Kearns, David, 93
Know your audience, 23–24
Koslowski, Dennis, 16

Language use
   grammar, 139–147

in-depth, 31
presentation, 31
   word choice, 53–56, 121–125
Leadership
   listening, 75
   qualities, 4, 45
   questioning, 75–76
Lebenthal, Mort, 12
Lecture/presentation *vs.* conversation, 111–119
Listening, 75
Lombardi, Vince, 51
Long presentation, breaking up, 131, 170

Marriott, J., Jr., 3
Matsushita, Konosuke, 65
Mattimore, Bryan, 74–76
McLuhan, Marshall, 90
McNeely, Scott, 5
McNerney, Jim, 70–71
Mediocrity, 4, 39
Memorable presentation, 98–99, 115–119
Merrill Lynch, 68–69
Mindstorming, 76
Mohammed, 17
Motorola, 66–68
Muscular words, 54–55
Mussolini, Benito, 16

99% Inspiration - Tips, Tales & Techniques for Liberating Your Business (Mattimore), 74
Nixon, Richard, 57

O'Neal, Stan, 68
Opening remarks, 127–131
Opportunities, look for, 44–45

Ordinary language, 53–56, 121–125
Orrick, David, 12

Packard, Dave, 71
Panasonic, 65
Parable, 133
Passion, 10, 165
Perception, 85
Personal story, 128
Pointers. See Checklist
POWER formula, 27–33, 115–117
Power word, 54–55
PowerPoint presentation, 149–161
Preparation, 25
Presentation
    attention-getting, 98–99, 115–119
    breaking up long, 131, 170
    conversation, compared, 111–119
    memorable, 98–99, 115–119
    PowerPoint, 149–161
    use of word, 31
Primal mind, 49–53
Project into the future, 60–61
Putnam Investments, 72

Questioning, 75–76
Quotation, 129

Regional dialect, 147
Reinforcement, 118
Rhetorical question, 129
Robo-speak, 53, 121–125

Scandals, 15–16
Scrushy, Richard, 16
Sense of purpose, 91
Shorter words, 54–56

Simplicity
    bottom line, 57–61, 115–117
    Edison, Thomas, 137
    18-minute wall, 131
    slide presentation, 149–161
    word choice, 53–56, 121–125
Sinclair, Chris, 134
Slide presentation, 149–161
Slides, 111–112, 167–168
Sloppiness, 38
Small potatoes, 143–147
Speed bumps (cautionary tale), 77–81
Stage fright, 170
Stalin, Joseph, 16
Star (winner's circle), 95–99
Starting strongly, 57–61, 115–117
Stealth bombs, 141–142
Stewart, Martha, 12–14
Story-telling, 128–129, 133–138
Syms, Sy, 12

Taming the Conflict Dragon (Hiam), 102
3M, 70–71
Tips. *See* Checklist
Toogood, Granville, 178
Trump, Donald, 86
Turner, Ted, 93
Tyco International, 16

Uncertainty, 36

Value added, 21–22
Visual aids, 149–161

Wal-Mart, 69–70

Walton, Sam, 69
Weak word *vs.* power word, 54–55
Welch, Jack, 8–9
White-collar renegades, 16
Who Says Elephants Can't Dance?
    (Gerstner), 66
Winner's circle (star), 95–99
W.L. Gore & Associates, 135

Word choice, 53–56, 121–125
Word slides, 112
Work-home balance, 89–91
WorldCom, 16

Xerox, 93

Zander, Ed, 66–67

ABOUT THE AUTHOR

Granville N. Toogood is America's top executive communications coach, a lecturer, seminar leader, best-selling author, cofounder of the Liminal Group in New York, and president of the Transformative Leadership Forum, a global professional development enterprise. He is a former news producer of the "Today Show," a TV journalist, *LIFE* magazine writer, and author of *The Articulate Executive*, *The Inspired Executive*, and *The Creative Executive*. He has coached more than half of the Fortune 100 CEOs, plus thousands of managers, senior executives, business leaders, elected officials, athletes, and celebrities all over the world. www.toogoodassoc.com; gtoogood@toogoodassoc.com